WEATHERING FOR
RAILWAY MODELLERS

Volume 1 - Locomotives and Rolling Stock

WEATHERING FOR RAILWAY MODELLERS

Volume 1 - Locomotives and Rolling Stock

GEORGE DENT

THE CROWOOD PRESS

First published in 2017 by
The Crowood Press Ltd
Ramsbury, Marlborough
Wiltshire SN8 2HR

www.crowood.com

British Library Cataloguing-in-Publication Data
A catalogue record for this book is available from the British Library.

ISBN 978 1 78500 330 1

Acknowledgements
For the supply of tools, paints and materials, my sincere thanks go to Alex Medwell and Lisa
Munro at The Airbrush Company, Alan Taylor at Modelmates, John Peck at Precision Labels,
and John Bristow at Deluxe Materials. Thanks also to Richard Foster, Chris Leigh, Mike
Harris and Chris Nevard at *Model Rail* magazine.

I'd also like to thank Jeanne Carr for her hospitality in Settle, where the first draft of this
book was written, along with the mysterious cat who kept me company as I typed furiously.
And, of course, a big shout out to all members of the Dent Collective, especially J-M –
thanks Duckie!

This book is dedicated to the memory of Pep. Sleep tight, little sausage.

Frontispiece
Small details, such as using washes on the light surrounds and the masked wiper trails, combine
to raise the level of realism.

Typeset by Jean Cussons Typesetting, Diss, Norfolk

Printed and bound in India by Parksons Graphics

CONTENTS

1   WHY WEATHER?   7

2   PAINTS, WASHES AND DRY PIGMENTS   14

3   TOOLS AND PREPARATION   21

4   WAGONS: FIRST FORAYS   30

5   WAGONS: NEXT STEPS   39

6   AIRBRUSHING: THE BASICS   50

7   AIRBRUSHING IN PRACTICE   63

8   TURNING TO DUST: CEMENT AND SCRAP WAGONS   72

9   RUST IN PEACE: PART ONE   80

10   RUST IN PEACE: PART TWO   88

11   RUST IN PEACE: PART THREE   94

12   TIMBER WORKS   100

13   SHADY TECHNIQUES   106

14   COACHING STOCK: PART ONE   114

15   COACHING STOCK: PART TWO   123

16	**MULTIPLE UNITS**	**132**
17	**DIESEL AND ELECTRIC TRACTION: PART ONE**	**143**
18	**DIESEL AND ELECTRIC TRACTION: PART TWO**	**152**
19	**DIESEL AND ELECTRIC TRACTION: PART THREE**	**162**
20	**STEAM TRACTION: PART ONE**	**174**
21	**STEAM TRACTION: PART TWO**	**183**
22	**STEAM TRACTION: PART THREE**	**192**
23	**STEAM TRACTION: PART FOUR**	**200**
	LIST OF SUPPLIERS	**206**
	INDEX	**207**

CHAPTER ONE

WHY WEATHER?

Weathering is a blanket term for a myriad of techniques aimed at making our models appear more realistic. While many assume it refers solely to the act of throwing dirty paints on to a surface, there is actually far more to it than that.

Adding highlights, shading and faded livery colours is all part of the weathering process. So, too, is the creation of authentic textures, burnishing, wood-grain effects, and peeling or worn paint finishes. Even the art of 'bulling up' a locomotive – recreating highly polished paintwork – can be classed as weathering. These processes also serve to bring out the best of a model's profile and detail relief. Indeed, even a seemingly basic or bland budget model can be transformed into something eye-catching.

Everything, be it a train, building, tree, car or even a human being, displays some degree of weathering. It might be ingrained dirt, water staining or a tatty pair of jeans, but if you look closely at any object,

there are bound to be shadows visible in a recess, a highlight created by sunlight catching a surface, or damp fungus growing on a tree trunk. Indeed, training our eyes to look more closely at an object and appreciating textures, tones and sheens – not simply 'counting the rivets' – is a useful skill. It can also become an obsession: I still find it difficult to walk past a rotten shed door, murky stone wall or greasy fuel tank without being inspired!

Weathering isn't just about making something look dirty: it's a means of helping objects blend into their surroundings, be it a train, car, building or human figure.

ABOVE: **There are countless weathering processes and materials to help create a range of textures and tones.**

RIGHT: **Freight stock can be treated in such a way that its purpose can be surmised even if the wagons are empty. A fine layer of limestone dust covers this train as it heads back to the quarries of the Peak District.**

THE TRAINS

Objects that spend their lives outdoors, operating in harsh environments, are likely to weather quickly and extensively. Railways have always provided a tough proposition for traction and rolling stock, from the steam age to the modern high-speed network. Exposure to the weather through all seasons, staining from exhausts, fuel, lubricants and brake dust, and the constant buffing and scraping from human traffic, all take their toll. Freight wagons, loaded and unloaded daily with anything from bitumen to coal, cement or limestone, take a real battering, which is reflected in their outward appearance.

Contrasting sheens are just as important as fine misted layers of dirt. Note how the shiny red carriage sides offer a counterpoint to the dusty underframes and roofs, just like the real thing.

The sides are mostly clean, but the grilles and recesses feature dark shading, and the dusty edges of the roof are distinctive. There's also plenty of tonal variation in the blue livery. Closer inspection reveals footprints in the dirt, from fitters clambering over the roof!

Despite regular cleaning, trains quickly regain a range of gritty and oily deposits. Note the ingrained dirt visible on the yellow ends and the dusty bonnet tops, which appear to be cleaned less frequently than the sides and ends.

A multi-layered approach to weathering creates a more visually interesting and realistic finish.

TOP LEFT: **An ostensibly clean Class 60. But closer scrutiny reveals plenty of streaks emanating from the roof, dirt and scuffs around the cab door, and deposits of grime on the bogies and underframe. Training your eye to search for these features is part of the weathering skill set.**

TOP RIGHT: **The other end of the same locomotive reveals peeling paint and corroded steel on the roof line, and more concentrated streaking and greasy stains around the fuel tank.**

MIDDLE: **Even well tended, preserved steam traction offers plenty of textural contrasts for us to capture. The finish on the smokebox is visibly flatter than the shiny tanks and cylinders, and there's even a small patch of rust near the hinges. Ingrained dirt on the otherwise clean bufferbeams brings out the detail in the rivet heads.**

BOTTOM: **There are more extreme examples that we can recreate, with areas of corrosion and peeling paint easy to reproduce using some innovative materials and methods.**

Many vehicle types feature characteristic weathering, such as oil tanks with dirty stains down the barrel. But this example also boasts traces of old brandings and plenty of chipped paintwork.

Looking as if it has been the target in a paintball shootout, this aggregates wagon has plenty of tones and textures worth capturing.

While the most prestigious trains were traditionally cleaned on a regular basis, it doesn't take long to accrue more dead flies on the windscreens, and exhaust staining or dust and grime on the underframes. The less glamorous passenger trains, especially in the post-1960s world, were generally less well cared for, in terms of outward appearances.

Weathering also helps us to place railway vehicles in specific places and times, as well as giving them a distinct identity. Traction and rolling stock near the end of its life needs to be portrayed as such, with shabby paintwork, corrosion and leaking oil, while newer types can offer a convincing contrast in sheen and cleanliness. The depot or branchline 'pet' locomotive, polished and fussed over by its crew, will also have a character all of its own, with a greasy patina from years of cleaning with oily rags. Similarly, freight vehicles ought to wear the scars of carrying their intended burdens, such as coal, iron ore or stone, identifying their purpose even if they're empty.

THE BOOK

This volume aims to share the results of my experiments in weathering over the past twenty or so years. I must have been about thirteen when I first began distressing and dirtying my rolling stock, using Humbrol enamel paints. My memory gets hazy these days, but I seem to recall that the impetus came from building a couple of plastic rally-car kits (a Peugeot 205 and a Lancia Delta!). My dad suggested I build a scenic diorama on which to display them, and with a muddy track forming the base, complete with puddles, it followed that the cars would have to be dirty too. Being a talented modeller himself, Dad gave me a few pointers, and having been satisfied with the results, I must have wondered if I could improve the locomotives and rolling stock on my model railway in a similar fashion. After all, I spent much of my youth watching grubby freight trains around Warrington, so my pristine recreations of the contemporary 1980s scene were not exactly accurate.

The dry-brushing method was an early staple, followed by the idea of painting the whole model in a filthy shade of brown/dark grey enamels and then wiping most of the paint away. This left traces and streaks of dirt behind, and the effect could be endlessly manipulated and refined until I was satisfied. Having happily started down the road to weathering, there was no turning back.

There are complex processes involved in weathering, but there are also plenty of simple techniques. Painting individual planks in slightly different shades prior to a weathering wash creates greater depth. Coloured pencils are great for mimicking burnished and exposed metalwork.

As well as the streaky deposits of dirt trapped in the planked bodywork, it's the small details, such as the less-than-perfect markings, that add extra realism.

Even amongst similar vehicle types, variety is important. If we weather them all identically, the overall picture will be spoilt.

There are plenty of quick ways of weathering wagons, with hand-applied paints and dry pigments ...

... or we can take things further and suggest ad hoc repairs and re-branding, telling the story of a hardworking vehicle that has passed through the workshops a few times.

THE CONTENT

This book is arranged in a number of loose sections, initially dealing with the theory behind the various paints, dry pigments and other weathering media, along with tools and application methods. The practical work begins with the onus on rolling stock, as this forms the ideal basis for developing aptitude and, more importantly, confidence. Most of the processes discussed in these early chapters are transferable to any railway (or non-railway) vehicle, in any scale and any country. Just because I have demonstrated one particular method on a British Railways coal wagon doesn't mean that it's not suitable for use on something completely different.

Looking at the prototype is an essential part of the weathering process. While I rarely seek to copy slavishly the characteristics of individual vehicles,

Areas of peeling paint bring plenty of interest to humble freight vehicles, revealing previous liveries and bare timber. Chapter 12 describes how effects like this can be captured in miniature.

For the ambitious, we can correctly structure a weathering job so that the rusty metal appears beneath the peeling paint, as it does in reality.

Pre-shading is a fascinating technique that looks difficult but can actually be easier than many other weathering tasks. It certainly helps to add life to an otherwise anonymous vehicle.

With a well-observed weathered finish, we can divert attention away from a model's shortcomings. This ancient Mainline 'Dean Goods' doesn't look so archaic at first glance, taking attention away from the terrible tender drive unit, complete with plastic wheels!

study of the real thing teaches us what effects are likely to appear on specific wagon, carriage or locomotive types in certain situations. There isn't the space to include many images of real trains in this book, as I have striven to give the reader as much practical advice as possible. Therefore, before embarking on a new project, do have a look at images of the real thing (or similar vehicles) to help you visualize the ends to which you'll be working. That is, if your primary concern is for prototype fidelity. Not everyone cares about such things, which I completely understand!

Weathering can also make a great model even better. This Hornby 'B1' will soon be transformed …

An intensive course in airbrushing is provided in Chapters 6 and 7, while this key weathering device crops up increasingly as the content becomes more advanced. Indeed, the projects in this book are arranged roughly in order of difficulty and can be followed from the beginning if desired, while modellers with some experience may be happy to dip in to specific chapters.

… into a later period Departmental locomotive. Most of the LNER livery remains under the many layers of airbrushed weathering, with just a few patches of BR lining and tender crest being applied in strategic areas.

With freight stock out of the way, we move on to the unique weathering characteristics of coaching stock, where different processes and aspirations are discussed. Motive power then follows, beginning with multiple units and some interesting ideas on filtering, fading and colour modulation. How do you make a train look shabby without making it dirty? This, and more, is revealed in Chapter 16.

Finally we get to the meaty subject of locomotives, and I have split the content between modern (diesel and electric) traction and steam locomotives. While both traction types share common processes up to a point, there are some methods that particularly suit steam subjects, such as recreating limescale stains, greasy connecting rods and coal dust.

Again, space and budget precludes the use of models to suit all countries, periods and scales, yet virtually everything featured in this book can be translated to any subject. All you need is to gain an understanding of the core practical principles, which can be endlessly tweaked and adapted to suit your own modelling tastes.

THE GOALS

Weathering can become addictive in many ways and the rewards are plenty, with great satisfaction to be had from a successful project. However, having created a more lifelike wagon, carriage or locomotive, the surroundings in which they operate will look incongruous unless they, too, are weathered. Indeed, a follow-up volume is being planned to deal with the subject of weathering buildings and scenery.

As well as describing and demonstrating a whole host of possible projects, materials and techniques, the ultimate goals of this book are to offer inspiration and encouragement, and to show just how much fun weathering can be.

CHAPTER TWO

PAINTS, WASHES AND DRY PIGMENTS

When I first got into weathering there was very little in the way of off-the-shelf products aimed at this pursuit. Instead, improvisation was essential, with regular hobby enamels and artists' pastels being pressed into use. While results were acceptable, there was a lot of unnecessary effort – and mess – involved. Happily, recent years have seen not only an upsurge in modellers' interest in weathering, but also in the variety of weathering media on offer. Products range from straightforward dry pigments (commonly known as weathering powders) and specific 'dirty' paint shades, to innovative 'chipping' formulas, realistic rust effects and weathering washes designed to be manipulated in various ways.

It's important to note that the majority of weathering products are not aimed solely at the railway hobby. Indeed, it pays to keep your eye on what may be happening in the worlds of aviation, military, figure and maritime modelling, as much of the innovation has originated from these communities. Furthermore, browsing through the wares of non-railway modelling stores is also recommended. Indeed, a good many of the products showcased throughout this book were discovered through my subscriptions to magazines such as *Airfix Model World*, *Scale Aviation Modelling*, *AFV/AIR Modeller* and *Military Illustrated Modeller*. I am also indebted to acquaintances in other modelling fields, who have informed me of certain new products and techniques.

Such is the untapped potential of the railway market, however, that paint and pigment brands have recently begun to add rail-themed products to their ranges. LifeColor, AK Interactive and MIG Productions are cases in point, while even Humbrol and Revell have been increasingly pitching their weathering products towards railway enthusiasts.

Inevitably, a wealth of choice makes informed decision more difficult. Therefore, one of the aims of this book is to provide readers with an understanding of the possibilities offered by a range of different products. Of course, you can find these things out for yourself via experimentation – which is how I have developed most of my favoured techniques. Or you can save time, and learn from my mistakes instead of your own!

PAINTS

Paint comes in various formulas, with the two main types being enamels and acrylics. I also employ artists'-style oil paints, which offer longer drying times

There are plenty of weathering paints to choose from, in enamel and acrylic formulas.

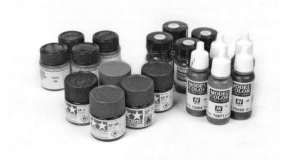

For most projects, only four or five paint shades are required.

and more scope for manipulation after application. The working characteristics and benefits of specific paints and finishes will be explained in detail over the following chapters, as their use occurs. Here, though, we will take a quick look at some of the fundamental features of the materials that I commonly employ.

ENAMELS

Enamels are probably the most popular type of hobby paint amongst railway modellers; they are solvent based and produce a superior, hardwearing finish, albeit with slow drying times (six to twelve hours). Adhesion is usually good on all surfaces, and the finish can be manipulated or removed with the aid of white spirit or enamel thinners, up to several hours after application. Note that the paints can be toxic (some brands may contain lead) and are highly flammable, so they must be used with care. When spraying, in particular, steps must be taken to avoid inhaling the fumes.

Well known brands offering enamels suitable for weathering include Humbrol, Revell, Phoenix Precision and RailMatch. The latter brand has been my default enamel of choice for decades; the screw-top glass jars and low viscosity are well suited to airbrushing work, without the need for too much thinner, which gives them a great advantage as far as I'm concerned. A new range of enamels emerged from Alclad2 while this book was being prepared, designed for airbrush use without the need for thinning. Having tested them extensively, they have certainly proved effective, although the range was fairly limited in terms of colours at the time of writing, being aimed initially at military modellers.

However, as is true of all brands, making a choice based on the actual colour of the paint, rather than what it says on the label, allows for a wide range of suitable weathering shades to be obtained. For example, a paint jar doesn't have to say 'locomotive frame dirt' in order to do the job. There are plenty of earthy browns and military camouflage colours that are more or less the same.

Special mention should be made of Humbrol's Metal Cote enamels. The unique formulation allows

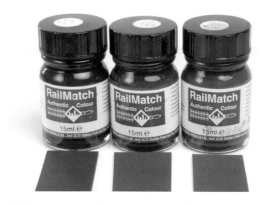

Different brands have alternative descriptions, but the three weathering shades most commonly employed in my work are (from left to right) Weathered Black, Roof Dirt and Frame Dirt.

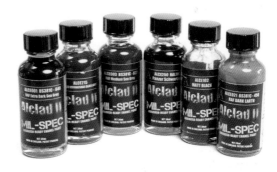

Alclad2's Mil-Spec enamels come pre-thinned, ready for airbrushing. A range of earthy browns, dark greys and blacks are available, albeit with military-themed descriptions.

Humbrol Metal Cote paints feature special ingredients that impart a realistic, greasy sheen.

for supremely realistic finishes to be created, not least as the dried paint can be buffed to simulate a metallic sheen. The gunmetal shade (27004) is perfect for use on steam locomotive underframes and valve gear, and is also great for portraying greasy deposits and streaking effects.

ACRYLICS

Acrylic paint formulas differ widely in their ingredients and performance. Tamiya's version, for instance, boasts a high alcohol content and behaves more like fast-drying enamels. On the other hand, those with water as the main ingredient, such as LifeColor and Revell Aqua, take longer to dry but offer little in the way of noxious fumes or toxic ingredients. Even the slower-setting acrylics are dry within an hour or two. Virtually all can be cleaned up with water before they've cured, and white spirit will usually shift them up to an hour or so after application, but after that, abrasives or drastic chemical intervention (model-paint stripper) may be required.

Apart from Tamiya paints, many acrylics struggle to adhere to glossy surfaces and factory finishes, especially once thinned and sprayed through an airbrush. Careful prior cleaning and degreasing is essential (as it is before any type of paint is applied), and I find that an overall enamel matt clear coat, applied via an aerosol or airbrush, provides an effective inter-

I am a great supporter of LifeColor acrylics, especially for hand-brushing work. The range of weathering shades is vast and many themed packs are available, giving six shades for specific tasks. The 'Dirty Effects' pack, containing a trio of 'grease' shades, is fantastic.

Vallejo is another range of acrylics that I can recommend. Slightly thicker than LifeColor, the eye dropper-style bottles allow for easy decanting and mixing.

mediate layer on which acrylics will sit happily. Once dry, most acrylics offer a high resistance to oils and solvents, meaning that they can be used on working locomotive models with confidence.

Having been brought up on enamels, it took me a while to get used to acrylics. However, once I'd accepted the fact that they behave differently, I soon cast off my initial reservations and I'm glad that I persevered, as they offer many advantages over smelly, slow-drying enamels.

Tamiya acrylic paints are best suited to airbrushing, offering many of the advantages of enamels, along with faster drying times. For best results, use Tamiya's own thinners.

CLEAR COATS
AND LACQUERS

As will be explained in due course, clear coats play an important role in the weathering process, either helping to seal a finish or by adding specific effects, such as water stains or an oily patina. Most paint brands feature clear coats of some description. It's worth having a selection of matt, satin and gloss coats on hand to cater for a variety of situations.

My usual preference for clear coats is the Alclad2 range. These are formulated exclusively for airbrush use, and a wide selection of sheens is available, ranging from high gloss to flat matt. Their ben-

A clear coat is useful as a prelude to weathering with acrylics or dry powders, to aid adhesion or to refine the final sheen.

efits include a rapid drying time (thirty minutes) and their ability to adhere to any surface as long as it is clean and dry. They can be applied equally well over enamels, acrylics or factory finishes.

AEROSOLS

Although a number of paint manufacturers offer weathering shades in aerosol format, I only ever use them for scenic work (if at all). The inability to control the spray pattern makes them a rather crude method of application. Despite what some sceptics say, weathering scale models is a careful and precise process to which a spray can is not suited. However, aerosol-based clear coats are useful, as will be seen in later chapters.

DYES

The Modelmates range of weathering dyes is an intriguing alternative to traditional paints. A wide variety of shades is on offer, suited to a whole host of rolling stock situations. The water-based dye is safe for use on any material, and can be manipulated with a damp brush or cotton swab indefinitely; indeed, the finish only becomes permanent once a sealing clear coat has been applied. This workability is welcome, allowing for mistakes to be rectified,

or weathering layers to be built up and perfected before they are sealed with a blast of varnish from an aerosol or airbrush. Applied by hand brush or airbrush (where no thinning is necessary), they may, however, struggle to adhere to some factory finishes unless a coat of matt varnish is applied beforehand.

Modelmates' Rust Effect dyes are slightly different. They contain textured pigments that dry to an incredibly lifelike rendition of corroded metal. Applying several layers creates a coarse texture and a broad range of tones. Again, it can be streaked

Modelmates dyes offer a fast-drying and water-soluble alternative to paints.

and manipulated with a damp brush or swab before sealing with a clear coat prior to further weathering.

OIL PAINTS

Despite using artists' oil paints extensively in my art-school days, the thought of employing them on my model trains never occurred to me until I saw how effective they could be for weathering military vehicles. With slow drying times and the potential for easy manipulation, it is possible to run the paint into and around recessed or raised surface detail, helping to create more definition.

Tubes of oil paints are useful for a range of techniques. Most brands offer matching thinners.

Metallic paints help to highlight small detail fittings and to create a burnished effect. AK Interactive True Metal paints are wax based and can be applied with brushes or swabs. When dry, they can be polished to a life-like appearance.

A little oil paint goes a long way, with each tube lasting for years if looked after properly. It is also versatile enough to be used in a dilute form as a weathering wash, or in a thicker state for heavier grime deposits. Many useful shades are available, and intermixing is easy on a small palette.

So popular have oil paints become with modellers that a number of new brands have sprung up, such as Wilder, Abteilung and AK Interactive. Most can be thinned with white spirit or dedicated thinners, and drying times vary.

THINNING

It is good basic practice to employ the same brand of paint and thinners, to ensure complete compatibility. Through trial and error you'll probably find a few brands of thinner that work equally well with other brands of paint. But from the outset, it's best to err on the side of caution.

SHAKEN OR STIRRED?

All paints are a mixture of solid pigments suspended in a liquid solvent, and unless the jar is kept agitated, the pigment is liable to settle at the bottom. Therefore, all paints must be shaken or stirred before application. Read the label to find out what method is best for each brand or formula: for example, acrylics usually require both a stir and a shake, while it's often better just to stir enamels. Also, if a job is taking more than a few minutes, you may have to re-stir or re-shake the paint regularly to keep the pigment evenly dispersed.

WASHES

Weathering washes are basically diluted paints, optimized so that the pigments are evenly dispersed within the liquid medium, allowing it to flow freely across a surface. Washes come in enamel or acrylic versions, and can be applied effectively by hand (brush, swab, sponge or other means), or sprayed through an airbrush. Their translucent nature means that several layers of the same wash can be built up

The slow drying times of enamel-based weathering washes allow for easy manipulation. Glossy sheens are ideal for deposits of oil or grease.

LifeColor liquid pigments can be layered to create tonal and textural variety. A remover agent is provided to help manipulate or clean away the paint altogether. Apply by hand brush, sponge, swab or airbrush.

to create denser shades where necessary. Washes are great for enhancing raised and recessed detail such as grilles, louvres, panels and planking detail, and are also perfect for adding streaking effects, oil leaks and rust deposits.

COMPATIBILITY

Although not usually an issue when weathering, it is worth pointing out that some paints can react badly with others, especially if the previous layer has not dried completely. However, in general terms enamels can sit on a dry acrylic base, and vice versa. Allow enamels at least twenty-four hours and acrylics twelve hours to cure, before recoating with another formula. If in doubt, test on a scrap model first. Some lacquer-based paints will cause underlying finishes to blister, although Alclad2 clear lacquers are safe for use on enamel and acrylic finishes. Again, just be sure that all previous paint layers are completely dry.

Interestingly, most enamel weathering washes state that they are formulated for use over acrylic finishes. This is because, once dry, acrylic paints are impervious to most solvents, allowing the washes to be manipulated with extra thinners if necessary, without the risk of disturbing the paint beneath.

The liquid solvent within paint is the cause of compatibility issues, rather than the solid pigments. Given that weathering washes are formulated with a much higher content of liquid solvent, they are likely to cause issues if the finish beneath is not entirely dry.

DRY PIGMENTS

Weathering powders can create a wide variety of visual effects and textures, without the need for an airbrush or other expensive equipment. Areas of brake dust, smoke and exhaust staining are good examples, along with heavier deposits such as coal dust and ash. All that is needed is a selection of soft-bristled brushes, sponges and cotton swabs and a little imagination. I prefer dry pigments from MIG, Vallejo, Lifecolor, Darkstar and Alclad2, each being supplied in either screw-top or flip-top lids. These versatile pigments offer excellent quality, and each

Dry powders offer distinctive textures and effects. Liquid fixatives improve adhesion, or can be mixed with the pigment to create textured paints or pastes.

can be mixed with acrylic or enamel paints, or thinners, to create a textured finish. They will happily adhere to all but the glossiest surface in their natural, dry state, often without the need for any fixative agent. They can also be intermixed freely with each other.

A matt surface is nearly always preferable, and the following chapters offer a range of application tips to get the most from dry powders, either using them in isolation or as part of a more comprehensive, multi-material approach.

Fixative solutions are offered to complement most ranges of weathering powders. These can be brushed on beforehand, to act as a primer/surfacing agent, or sprayed on afterwards using an airbrush. Furthermore, they can be intermixed with dry pigments to create something resembling a weathering wash, or even a thick paste to secure thicker deposits.

OTHER MEDIA

Tamiya's range of Weathering Master packs, presented in cosmetic-style 'compact' packaging, offers an excellent resource. They can be used in a similar way to powders, brushed lightly on to a surface to create misting effects. Alternatively, by using a sponge applicator, they can be applied in heavier

deposits or as more pronounced streaking. They are also excellent for picking out raised detail, such as grilles and handrails, suggesting scuffing and the exposure of bare metal to burnishing or corrosion.

The oil-based pigments offer excellent adhesion and a permanent finish, although the staining can be altered or removed with white spirit. A twin-ended brush/sponge applicator is supplied with every pack. A greater range of effects can be obtained with other applicators, such as shaped cosmetic sponges, cocktail sticks and cotton swabs.

Now that we've looked into the most common forms of weathering materials, we ought to consider how best to prepare the models.

ABOVE: **Artists' coloured pencils, preferably the 'blendable' variety, have many uses, from highlighting raised detail to creating rust patches.**

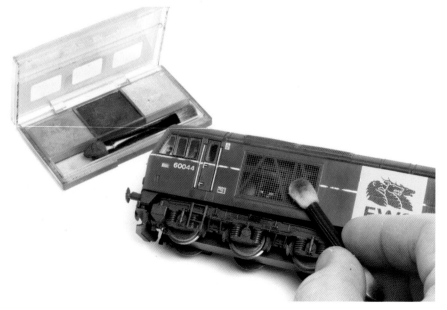

Tamiya's wax-based weathering compacts help to pick out raised detail and create subtle streaking effects.

CHAPTER THREE

TOOLS AND PREPARATION

Any modelling endeavour requires a minimum of tools and equipment, and weathering is no different. We need to ensure that we can dismantle – and reassemble – a model, as well as handle it effectively, while protecting it from damage. There is also the matter of how we apply the various weathering and masking mediums.

GENERAL TOOLS

It often helps to dismantle a model to some degree in order to make weathering tasks as straightforward as possible, so we'll need the right tools with which to part bodyshells from chassis, and to remove any small details that may be at risk of damage. Ready-to-run (RTR) models differ in how they're put together, but a set of miniature screwdrivers, of different sizes and patterns, will be essential. An array of stiff plastic shims, cut from plastic card and chamfered at one end, will help to prise bodies away from underframes in a less invasive manner than metal tools.

Some padding for the workbench is recommended. Also, bespoke locomotive cradles are available from various sources, allowing models to be retained securely while inverted. With both hands free, it's so much easier to remove or replace tiny mounting screws from awkwardly recessed areas. A regular assortment of holding and cutting tools will see plenty of use. A good quality knife is needed for cutting masking tapes and films. Tweezers of different sizes, and cocktail sticks, can help with masking and assembly tasks, as do fine-nosed pliers.

Abrasives are required for surface preparation, distressing, manipulating and corrective work. Albion Alloys, Flex-i-File, Micro Mesh and Squadron are brands you can trust, offering abrasives in the form of flexible sticks, pads, sheets and strips. A good assortment of each will be a worthwhile investment, with grades ranging from 4,000 to 12,000 grit.

Periodically clean your abrasives in soapy water to remove debris from the grit and to keep them working efficiently. Other implements for distressing or burnishing work include steel-wire brushes, old (but clean) toothbrushes, and glass-fibre scratch brushes.

FINISHING TOOLS

Tools for preparing paints and other weathering media are equally important. Paddle-shaped paint stirrers are most effective for dispersing pigments,

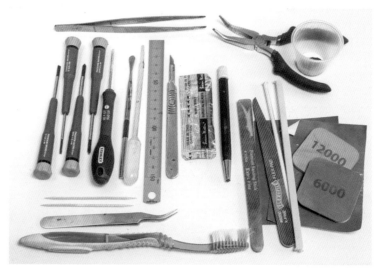

Only a small array of tools is required, mostly for the preparation and handling of the model.

while those with a spoon-shaped end are excellent for decanting small amounts of paint into a mixing jar or on to a palette.

Power stirrers are quicker at preparing paints, though they can make a mess if not used carefully. Instead of buying a purpose-made power stirrer, I simply shaped a length of stiff wire – made from a coat hanger – into a spiral pattern. This is then mounted into a cordless mini-drill. The drill's speed is switched to the slowest setting to minimize the potential for inadvertently decorating the walls.

Pipettes for adding controlled amounts of thinners, plus a selection of mixing palettes and measuring cups, are necessities.

OTHER ESSENTIALS

Wearing disposable gloves while handling models will avoid the risk of depositing fingerprints in wet paint or freshly applied powders. They will also prevent contamination from the oils in our skin, which may hinder the adhesion of weathering media. Protection of the skin from harmful solvents is another point in their favour.

Be wary of talc-filled gloves because although they offer greater comfort, the powder is likely to be on the outside, too. Therefore, after putting on a fresh pair of gloves, wipe your hands on a damp cloth to ensure they're clean.

Fume extraction is discussed in Chapter 6, but wearing a facemask is recommended when spraying paints using an airbrush or aerosol. It is also important to avoid inhaling the ultra-fine dust from weathering powders, so wherever possible, work in a well-ventilated area, especially when using solvent- or alcohol-based paints, washes and thinners.

We need plenty of light to work in; natural light is preferable, but daylight-simulating bulbs are the next best thing. The model should be illuminated clearly from more than one angle, so that we can judge colours and shades correctly. It is very easy to overdo the various weathering techniques due to poor lighting.

Finally, be prepared to get through plenty of tissue to mop up spillages, and clean work surfaces and paintbrushes, palettes and mixing vessels. Kitchen towel works out expensive, so consider large rolls of decorator's tissue from hardware or DIY stores.

APPLICATORS

The weathering media must somehow be applied to the models, and there are numerous options. Paintbrushes offer the obvious starting point. Various shapes and sizes will be required, although I find that 'flatties' are most used. Weathering can be damaging to the health of brushes, although good-quality ones tend to last longer. Natural sable bristles are preferred, but these can be expensive. Some synthetic bristles are all right, but it's important to choose carefully; Humbrol's newer brushes are good for the rougher jobs, while those offered by Tamiya, Revell and other well-known model brands are worth trying.

My personal choice is LifeColor's range of high-quality sable brushes. Alas, they are not cheap, but they last a long time if maintained sympathetically. Expo Tools have recently released a set of angled flat brushes, aimed directly at dry-brushing techniques, and these are very effective. Fine-tipped round brushes will be required for intricate work, such as adding delicate streaking effects or picking out small details.

I tend to keep separate stocks of brushes for painting, dry-brushing, and the application of weathering powders. The latter two undertakings can quickly

A good selection of paintbrushes, of varying shapes and sizes, is essential.

ruin a brush, so I have a cascade system, where the best and newest brushes are reserved for high-grade painting work. Once they start showing signs of wear and tear, they are put into the weathering pot, initially for use with washes and paints, before eventual demotion to the least precise jobs. Having said that, for delicate dry-brushing or powder application, the brushes must be in good condition.

Look after your brushes and you'll get more work out of them. Clean the bristles thoroughly after each job, and don't leave them standing in jars of water or thinners for more than a few minutes. Acrylics can injure brushes more than enamels, contrary to what many modellers assume, as their fast-drying nature makes the paint harder to remove. Adopt the good habit of rinsing a brush in water every few minutes when working with acrylics (or thinners when using Tamiya acrylics) to prevent the paint drying on the bristles. The same goes for enamels, too, especially as many modern formulas contain rapid drying ingredients, so a quick swill in white spirit or suitable thinners will benefit a brush's health and the quality of your work.

At the end of a session, pamper the brushes with a 'shampoo and set'. This doesn't mean an elaborate hairdo, but a quick lather in regular shampoo will remove any residues of paint, pigment and thinners. After rinsing in clean water, the bristles can be re-shaped and left to dry. Brush soaps are also available for this task, avoiding the need to raid the bathroom cabinet. This extra cleansing is especially effective with sable-haired brushes, encouraging the natural material to retain its flexibility and soft texture.

Microbrushes, available in numerous sizes and shapes, are a real boon for delivering small amounts of paint into awkward areas. They are also ideal for creating controlled streaking or smudging effects. The sponge-tipped versions are excellent for dry-brushing work, such as burnishing handrails and the edges of small components, where an ordinary brush would be too cumbersome. Their precise nature and ability to retain small amounts of fluid also makes them very useful for cleaning jobs, especially removing paint, debris and unwanted residues from wheels and electrical contacts.

Prolong the life of your brushes by cleaning them thoroughly and re-shaping the bristles after use. Treat with shampoo or dedicated brush soap. Deluxe Materials' Brush Magic shifts stubborn paint deposits and revives brushes seemingly past their best.

Other means of applying weathering paints and washes include natural and synthetic sponges, the former offering a more random array of textures. Sponges are excellent for creating rust and corrosion effects in a number of ways: see Chapters 8, 9 and 10 for more details.

SWABS

Cotton buds – or swabs – will see plenty of use throughout this book, employed in a number of ways. Their main use is for manipulating paints and washes after application. They are also well suited to cleaning and degreasing the subject beforehand, and treating the wheels afterwards.

Choose good-quality 100 per cent cotton swabs, such as Johnson's baby buds, as they retain their shape and fibres better than cheaper brands. Moreover, budget buds tend to disintegrate rapidly, revealing the end of the plastic shaft, which can scuff or scratch the model's surface. In addition, if the shaft is too flexible, it's difficult to retain full control of the swab. Modellers in the USA have the option of Q-tips, which are more effective than many cheaper brands of swab aimed at cosmetic or baby use.

While standard cosmetic cotton buds are essential for many weathering tasks, higher grade swabs, as offered by Tamiya, are also worth the investment.

Generic buds are fine for most tasks, but there are occasions when a narrower point or a more resilient cotton pad is required. Packs of cosmetic buds offer different sizes and shapes, but if, like me, you are shy of queuing at a make-up counter, Tamiya offers some superior swabs in a variety of shapes and sizes. While they're not cheap, they are of a very high quality and will last a lot longer than cheaper alternatives. Less prone to leaving behind stray fibres, these cotton pads also retain their shape, making them suitable for more precise tasks. Used sparingly, a pack will last for countless weathering projects, so they are a worthwhile luxury.

CLEANLINESS IS A VIRTUE

A surface needs to be clean and free of greasy contaminants before any paints or pigments can adhere properly, so it is important to ensure that models are correctly prepared. There is little point in spending hours applying a weathered finish only for it to be wiped away as soon as the model is handled for the first time. Indeed, we want our works of art to last the course and survive years of operation.

It is rarely possible to give a model a good wash before weathering, as we're usually dealing with fully assembled locomotives and rolling stock. But if it is possible, a good scrub with a mild detergent will shift most unwanted residues and debris. Avoid washing-

up liquids, as they contain ingredients designed to leave a shine on your crockery and moisturize your skin. General purpose cleaners, such as Flash or Cif (in the UK), will suffice, but be sure to rinse the model thoroughly with clean water and then allow it to dry completely.

Alcohol-based cleaners can be used safely around electrical and mechanical components, meaning that models can be left intact if need be. Isopropyl alcohol (IPA), sometimes referred to as 'rubbing alcohol', is a mild solvent that is nonetheless effective on oils, greases and other contaminants. Different formulas exist, and those explicitly marketed as safe on plastics and painted finishes must be chosen. A number of products are offered with modelling and craft use in mind, such as Just Like the Real Thing's Model Clean. Medea's Body Art formula, which is marketed for fingernail art purposes, is just as useful on plastic and metal models.

Apply the IPA sparingly with a clean brush, and then wipe it away with cotton swabs. It takes a few applications to ensure complete cleanliness: I follow the dictate that one application loosens the dirt, the second removes it and a third makes sure. Underframes and chassis, where oil and grease deposits will be thicker, may need further applications before all residues are removed. Don't forget

Alcohol cleaners, tailored for use on models, will help prepare surfaces before weathering.

to swill the brush in the alcohol between each application, to avoid spreading the grease around the surface. After the final cleanse, allow the model to dry out for a few hours, and from this point on, avoid handling it with your bare hands if possible.

DISMANTLING

Breaking a locomotive, carriage or wagon into component parts often makes for easier handling. Simply popping the wheels out of a coach or wagon underframe will allow them to be treated, and then cleaned, more effectively. It also solves the issue of the model rolling away!

Separating the body from the chassis also helps, then mounting the bodyshell on to a sprung painting stand; this keeps both hands free and minimizes the risk of contaminating wet paint with fingerprints or smudges. Underframes, with their complex relief, can be treated more effectively in isolation, ensuring even coverage around all the raised and recessed detail. Indeed, underframes tend to gather much more dirt on a daily basis and are less likely to be cleaned as often as the sides and ends of a vehicle; therefore treating the two elements individually allows for a different approach and alternative materials to be employed.

There is no need to go to too much trouble with dismantling; simply removing one or two smaller

detail fittings to ensure better access for paintbrushes or swabs can make a big difference. Tank wagons, for example, with ornate walkways and ladders, can prove challenging when weathering with an airbrush. Ensuring that the paint reaches partially obscured yet highly visible spaces is not easy; moreover, perforated walkways and ladders create a stencilling effect on the surface below. This is not an insurmountable issue, but it is a factor that often leads to more weathering being applied than may be desired.

So it may be a good idea to remove the walkways and ladders temporarily while the problem areas are treated to the desired extent. The separated parts can be weathered in isolation, before re-fitting. However, it is vital to ensure that the overall model will appear coherent once it has been put back together. Using the same shades of paints, washes and powders is essential if the parts are to sit side by side, and a degree of 'blending' work will still be necessary after reassembly.

While the above relates mostly to rolling stock, locomotives often pose a greater challenge, as the nature of the prototype and how the model has been constructed dictates how readily it can be broken down into manageable chunks.

If dismantling will be too much hassle, or poses too great a risk of damage, then the model can be treated as it is. Masking will be required, and

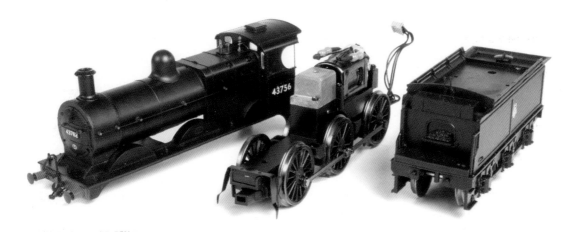

Dismantling a model makes it easier to handle and allows full access to the wheels and chassis.

Some separate details are best installed before weathering. Others, especially the more delicate fittings, are best left until later.

handling the model may be more complicated, but it saves having to reattach wires, diagnose faults and reinstate tiny details. With steam traction, it is often the wheels that cause the most difficulties, as they need to be treated evenly to avoid a patchy appearance. Furthermore, spoked wheels reveal glimpses of the frames behind, which also need treating.

We must also be wary of compromising electrical power transmission or the free movement of mechanical components. The chapters dedicated to steam locomotive weathering (see Chapters 20–23) reveal a number of ways in which these problems can be addressed.

Another factor to consider before work starts is whether or not to fit small detail parts that may be supplied with a model. The same goes for kit-built locomotives and stock, where delicate protrusions such as radio aerials, lamp brackets, windscreen wipers, headboards and fire irons are often best weathered separately and installed later. Much depends on the degree and type of weathering envisaged, as to what will be at risk of damage. Items such as brake rodding and bufferbeam pipes

and hoses may demand a gentler physical approach during weathering, but their presence from the start will at least ensure consistency.

MASKING

A number of different masking materials are employed in my workshop, with low-tack tapes,

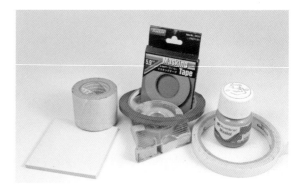

Keep a stock of good quality, low-tack masking tapes at hand. Tamiya and Tristar are trusted brands. Masking film, fluid and post-it notes are also useful.

Liquid masking fluid eases the task of protecting glazing and headlights. For larger apertures, roughly cut a piece of tape to sit in the centre of the pane, and seal the rest of the window with fluid. Application is best with a cocktail stick.

The fluid will dry to a flexible film that can be peeled away after the weathering work is complete.

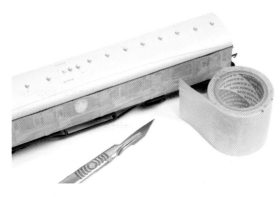

When cutting masking tape or film, always use a fresh scalpel blade.

Very large models, such as 'O'-gauge locomotives, demand a lot of space, so ensure that the workbench is free from clutter. Improvising a means of jacking up the model on a turntable to a comfortable working height may be necessary – just make sure that it's secure!

Mounting the model at a comfortable working height is important, especially when working with an airbrush. Excessive handling is undesirable, so the use of a turntable is preferred, extended with scraps of timber to cope with longer vehicles. Blobs of Blu Tack or strip wood will prevent stock rolling away.

If parts are treated separately, clamps and mini-vices can be employed to hold them firmly while the weathering is carried out.

Rolling-stock wheels are easier to treat remotely from the vehicle, allowing the rims and bearing surfaces to be cleaned effectively. Wooden clothes-pegs are made to measure for 'OO' wheelsets!

films and masking fluids being the most common. Less obvious options include post-it notes, Blu Tack and hand-held stencils shaped from scraps of card. The choice of masking media is dictated by the demands of particular weathering methods, as well as the properties of the model at hand. Protecting glazing is the commonest task prior to weathering, and again, the application method depends on the vehicle. Passenger carriages will often have their entire sides masked up with single strips of wide tape, while locomotives are more likely to have their individual panes covered with tape and/or masking fluid.

Masking offers the opportunity to keep certain areas cleaner than others, which is helpful in many situations. After applying the heaviest deposits of muck where it is needed, the masking can be removed and the 'cleaner' areas treated in a more understated fashion. Masking will also protect mechanical components such as motors, gears and bearings, as well as electrical contacts or circuit boards.

One point to remember is that it is best to remove the masks as soon as possible to avoid any unwanted residues being left behind.

CLEAN WHEELS

Ensure that all wheels, especially those collecting power, are kept spotlessly clean. Dirty wheels will deposit debris on to the tracks, so it makes sense to do the job properly. Avoid using abrasives, however tempting this can sometimes be. White spirit should also be avoided as it can leave behind a sticky film, encouraging dirt to accumulate. It is far better to use a liquid cleaner such as Track Magic from Deluxe Materials, which is very effective on wheels and electrical contacts. Cleaning is easier while the paint is fresh, but Track Magic will shift long-dried paint with a little extra work with a cotton swab or microbrush. Treat the wheel tread, flanges and the rear faces, especially if wiper pickups bear against them.

After completing a weathering job on a locomotive or multiple unit, and cleaning the wheels and contacts, it is important to re-lubricate moving parts and give the model a thorough test run. Valve gear and connecting rods need re-oiling, along with axles, wheel bearings and any gears that may have been de-greased earlier. It is vital that our models run as well as they look!

All wheels and electrical contacts should be cleaned after weathering. A foam-lined cradle will protect the finished model while cleaning.

In order to reach around locomotive wheels, especially on steam-outline models, a 9-volt battery can be employed to quickly 'jog on' the motion by touching the two terminals on to the wheels of a 'OO' locomotive. This is not suitable for DCC-fitted models.

A quick and effective wheel-cleaning tool is offered in various gauges by Trix. Taking power from the tracks, the brass brushes can be loaded with cleaning fluid.

CHAPTER FOUR

WAGONS: FIRST FORAYS

A number of projects are suggested here, each offering a gentle introduction to weathering. We'll be concentrating on freight rolling stock to begin with, due to the lower cost and risk factors: far better to make mistakes on a £20 wagon than on a £200 locomotive! There is also far less complexity with freight stock, with little in the way of dismantling, or electrical and mechanical parts to worry about. The stress factor can be reduced still further by employing old, scrap or second-hand models. Even if you never intend to run them on your layout, they'll provide a perfect three-dimensional test-bed. And they can always be cleaned up, repainted and treated again.

Three of the core weathering mediums are explored here: weathering washes, dry pigments and regular paints. Washes and powders offer a unique range of effects and, as we discussed in Chapter 2, the three materials each have their own strengths and limitations.

A dark wash will bring out the relief without necessarily making the vehicle look dirty. Planked wagons are an ideal example: simply brush on a small amount of the wash, then wipe away the excess with a cotton swab, leaving the pigment to sit in the recesses.

WASHES

With heavily diluted pigments, washes are excellent for adding shading and grime to recessed areas. Most of the medium can be wiped away, leaving raised surfaces as clean or grubby as desired. In this respect, they can bring life to an ex-works vehicle, or help to portray a thoroughly unkempt version.

When applied in multiple layers, washes bring greater depth and tonal variety to a surface, especially when different wash shades are employed, although each layer must be dry before further coats are added. They are also useful in other ways, perhaps adding a contrasting, greasy sheen to an otherwise dusty matt finish.

Some washes may struggle to adhere to gloss surfaces, while matt finishes are rougher and will capture much more of the pigment. This can be great for producing heavily weathered vehicles, but the creation of subtle effects may be difficult. Satin surfaces, being a halfway house between gloss and matt, are preferable in most instances as the behaviour of the washes is easier to control.

Water-based washes are excellent on matt surfaces and porous materials such as wood or card. Conversely, they can be unpredictable on glossier surfaces and RTR finishes, although a coat of matt varnish beforehand solves the problem. Enamel washes can be manipulated freely for hours after application, and are particularly recommended for use over acrylic and RTR finishes. If applying enamel washes over enamel paints, allow at least forty-eight hours for the previous layers to dry out completely.

Regular paint formulas can be converted to washes simply by thinning with a compatible solvent. Avoid fast-drying airbrushing thinners when working with enamels, as these are too aggressive. Opting for good-quality white spirit (known as mineral spirits in the USA) will suffice, while many ranges of wash include a suitable, gentle thinner formula, such as MIG, AK Interactive or Abteilung.

APPLYING WASHES

Washes need to be shaken and stirred thoroughly, before and during use, to ensure that the pigment is evenly dispersed. For overall coatings, use a soft-bristled flat brush, working the fluid into all the recesses. I tend to work on a small area at a time, say, two or three square inches. Once the wash is in place, take a dry cotton swab and gently wipe away any excess in vertical strokes, relative to the model's height. Any streaking that is produced will mimic the effects of rain and gravity.

You can leave as much or as little wash on the surface as you desire. However, it is only once the medium starts to dry out that you get an accurate picture of how the surface will appear. This is another point in favour of enamel washes, as you can go back to the model an hour or two later and make adjustments with a swab dipped in white spirit or a matching formula of thinners.

For a more targeted approach, a fine brush can be dipped in the wash and then place it on the model. The wash will flow into the recess through a combination of capillary action and gravity. Any excess is then carefully wiped away with a fine swab or a clean brush dipped in thinners. This method is known as pin washing, and will be discussed in more detail in later chapters.

Build up several layers, allowing each to dry, to create more tonal variety. Use the brush's bristles to introduce streaking effects.

Try a number of different shades to add variety. Some washes will struggle to show up on a black underframe, but 'rust' shades often do. These are also great for picking out detail fittings susceptible to corrosion.

A handful of MIG washes have been employed to bring this Bachmann model to life, greatly enhancing the surface relief. Certain areas, however, such as the underframe and interior, lack a suitably dusty texture.

Choosing a suitable shade of wash depends as much on the model's livery as on the planned extent of weathering. Rich livery elements, such as dark red, brown and blue, will need darker washes in order for them to be visible. Lighter liveries, such as grey, cream or yellow may require lighter wash shades. MIG's Neutral Wash, for instance, is perfect for white or pale surfaces, imparting a greyish tint and thus avoiding too stark a contrast.

If the paint proves difficult to remove, try dipping the swab in a little white spirit; this will be effective on acrylics and enamels.

For a more pronounced, dirty appearance to planked vehicles, try creating your own thick wash from regular paints. Here, LifeColor acrylics have been mixed to create a dirty, dark brown shade, which is applied to a small area of the model at a time.

The wash shade can also be tailored to the wagon's purpose. Coal- and coke-carrying vehicles, for example, are likely to be stained primarily with black coal dust, so darker washes are more appropriate, regardless of the vehicle's livery. Iron-ore wagons will similarly benefit from orangey-red-brown washes to match the distinctive hue of the mineral. To avoid too uniform an appearance, whatever loads or liveries are involved, apply more than one wash shade. Either mix a few washes together or build up a number of light, individual layers, allowing each to dry thoroughly.

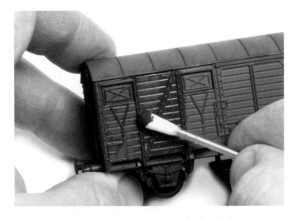

Then immediately wipe away the bulk of the paint with cotton swabs, working in vertical strokes. Remove as much or as little paint as you like until the desired effect is created. This brush-on, wipe-off technique will occur throughout this book, employed in many different ways.

Treating black underframes with paints will be far more successful than washes alone. Stipple the paint into all the nooks and crannies, removing the excess with swabs.

Although washes may be versatile, their lack of opacity makes them less effective on darker surfaces. Black underframes, in particular, can be too challenging for many washes. I've managed to gain some near-acceptable results with MIG enamel washes on underframes, but they required multiple applications and the finished result didn't truly reflect the nature of the prototype. Underframes are dusty places, and for a more authentic effect we need the unique charms of dry pigments.

It is often more convenient to remove the wheels and treat them separately. Keep the paint off the pinpoint axles.

If any paint strays on to the rims and flanges, wipe it away with a swab, being careful not to disturb the paint on the faces. Track-cleaning fluid and a micro applicator brush will take care of any stubborn paint deposits.

Treating van roofs is also recommended to dissemble the flat appearance of plastic or metal components. Here, a flat brush is applying a layer of LifeColor's acrylic Weathered Black in lateral strokes.

When dry, apply a dark wash over the roof and use swabs to remove the excess. Employ lateral strokes to create streaks in an authentic pattern.

POWDER PIGMENTS

Weathering powders offer a variety of potential uses, either employed on their own or in combination with other media. The finely ground pigment is excellent for creating dusty textures, and can be dispersed readily to create soft-edged effects. While initial application is best with soft-bristled brushes, dry pigments can be manipulated with stiffer brushes, or by swabs dipped in fixative solutions, to create streaking and smudging effects. Indeed, fixing solutions can be used to remove some or all of the pigment, as well as secure it.

There are two main drawbacks, however: powders are messy, and adhesion can sometimes be a problem. The first issue can be resolved by wearing gloves and protecting the work area with plenty of newspaper. Watch out for stray powders staining carpets and your clothing, too. As for adhesion, powders prefer a surface with a little 'bite'. Therefore, a matt surface is preferred, and it is recommended to treat the subject to a thin layer of matt varnish before weathering commences, especially for RTR models.

As with washes and paints, mixing a variety of shades avoids the risk of overly uniform, one-dimensional effects. Moreover, by concentrating darker tones into recesses or around raised details, the sense of depth and relief can be exaggerated. Be patient and apply several light layers of differing tones, brushing away the excess with a soft, dry brush. Resist the urge to blow the powder away with your breath, as the moisture will create unwanted staining.

If the streaks appear too pronounced, they can be toned down with lightly brushed dry pigments. For these vans I have mixed a little LifeColor Golan Dark Earth with MIG's Grimy Black.

Powders also bring a welcome dusty texture to the body and underframe. The powders will cling securely to the matt sheen from the previously applied acrylic paint. Mix a variety of shades on a palette before applying them to the model. Flat brushes with soft bristles offer the best results.

Once the powders have been applied, they can be manipulated slightly with a stiff-bristled brush (an old toothbrush is effective), creating further subtle streaking.

Raised details, such as door handles and brake gear, can be picked out with the tip of a coloured pencil. Try light grey, silver, umber or rusty red shades, as appropriate.

With more tonal and textural variety, and some authentic gravity-induced streaking, this wagon looks highly convincing.

A mix of paint washes and dry powders creates a fast, simple and effective way of bringing rolling stock to life, particularly in 'N' gauge.

By choosing the appropriate shades of paint and powders, we can simulate the peculiarities of specific commodities. This van is intended for carrying bagged cement, so a variety of grey pigment shades has been applied over a base of general weathering washes and paints.

The previous coats of acrylic paint, applied in the brush-on, wipe-off manner, give the powders plenty to cling to. The dusty sheen contrasts nicely with the cleaner areas of the bodywork.

If heavier grime deposits are necessary, brush on a fixative solution, and before it dries, stipple on a layer of powder, working it into and around the detail relief. Leave for thirty minutes or so before repeating the process, building up as many layers as you need until the desired results are obtained.

A quicker method is to mix the pigment with the fixative away from the model, creating a thin paste. Brush on to the model and allow it to dry, before building up further layers if necessary. The paste can be made thicker if desired, adding more pigment to create a slurry, which can be very effective for cement hoppers or aggregate wagon interiors. With these latter approaches the surface may appear patchy following the final application, so once the fixative has evaporated completely, dust it over with more dry pigments to soften the overall effect.

If you've been working on a matt surface, there should be no need for an overall coat of fixative to seal the powders in place. However, if there are concerns about the finish being disturbed, fixative solutions can be sprayed using an airbrush. Alternatively, a very light coat of matt varnish from a 'rattle can' is an option. Unfortunately the pressure

Powders, when used on their own, demand a matt surface to cling to. Off-the-shelf models benefit from an overall coat of matt varnish, applied using an aerosol. Remove or cover the wheels and any glazing beforehand.

For wagons with deeply ribbed bodies and a rich livery, start by brushing on a mix of black and grey powders, working the pigment into the corners of each rib.

from the aerosol is likely to blow away some of the powder and lessen the weathered effect. If this spoils your intended weathering, simply wait for the varnish to cure before adding a little more powder, which should adhere sufficiently to the matt surface without the need for further sealants.

MIDDLE LEFT: Then lightly brush away the excess pigment before dipping a swab into a fixative solution. The damp tip is then wiped over the recessed panels, keeping away from the edges as much as possible. The fixative actually loosens the pigment, allowing some or all of it to be removed, as desired. Leave the pigment in the recesses and against the sides of the ribs.

LEFT: Allow the fixative to dry before softening any hard edges with a lighter layer of powders, adding more tonal variety with different pigment shades. The underframe can be treated in a similar fashion.

In order to apply deeper deposits of powder in the interior, brush on a layer of fixative.

Before the fluid dries, stipple on plenty of pigment with a dabbing action, being sure to work into all the corners. When dry, brush out any loose material; repeat if necessary.

The detail relief of the finished MEA wagon has been enhanced by the dark pigments around the ribs. Pale grey and cream powders suit the vehicle's job of carrying limestone aggregates.

WHAT TO DO IF IT GOES WRONG

First, if it goes wrong, don't panic! Second, don't be disheartened – it happens to us all. Virtually all weathering products, including paints, can be removed shortly after application. We've already seen how pigment fixative solutions can be used to remove the powders altogether, if desired.

As for paints and washes, check the product's instructions, as some brands can be shifted with water, white spirit, methylated spirit or turpentine shortly after application. Enamel-based media offer a larger window of workability, while acrylics, which can be removed immediately with white spirit, may be difficult to shift once dry. Rather than reach for the model paint stripper, however, a project can often be salvaged with abrasives and a little imagination.

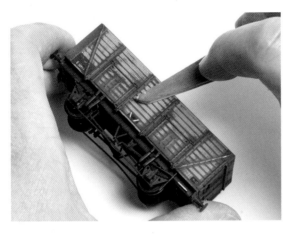

If you are unhappy with your early attempts at weathering, don't worry, as most materials can be removed before they dry completely. Even much later, paints can be shifted with fine abrasives. Indeed, they can also be used to rescue an aborted weathering job.

Having rubbed away most of the heavy-handed weathering with medium and fine abrasive strips, using vertical strokes to create streaking effects, 'dirty' deposits were left around the raised detail and in the recessed seams. Any hard edges to the weathering can then be smoothed with lightly applied powders.

It's not the weathered finish that I'd originally intended, but the abraded surface has imparted a very subtle texture, enhanced by the subsequent layers of dry pigment.

A GLIMPSE OF THE POSSIBLE

The projects showcased in this chapter have hopefully revealed the potential for transforming models using only simple materials and techniques. Detail relief has been enhanced while introducing authentic grimy and dusty textures. Each process, after a couple of practice runs, is quick to master and offers fast results.

CHAPTER FIVE

WAGONS: NEXT STEPS

Having explored a number of simple weathering tasks, we can now build on these foundations and go a little further in our quest for realism. As we have seen, plank detail provides the modeller with plenty of opportunities, regardless of how fancy the overall model is. Indeed, even elderly, basic models can be vastly improved with some careful applications of paint and pigment, taking the eye away from (albeit briefly) any shortcomings in terms of prototype fidelity. With this in mind, this chapter will look at a range of timber-bodied rolling stock from the steam and modern eras. We will also consider how steel-bodied wagons, with their smooth surfaces, can be enhanced with the addition of texture and tonal variations.

TIMBER TALES

Private owner, wooden-bodied minerals, general-purpose vans and open wagons were once the mainstay of railways around the world, carrying all manner of commodities. Designed for intensive use, often in filthy conditions, they rarely remained pristine, especially in the post-1945 era. Repairs to individual planks and partial repaints, or timber left untreated, were common, leading to a patchwork exterior effect. Wagon interiors were seldom painted, unless lined with a protective coating to cope with corrosive commodities. Yet RTR models feature one-dimensional interiors, either using the livery colour or with a vague attempt at a natural wood finish.

Recreating realistic timber grain effects is not as difficult as many modellers assume. Choosing the right colours and adopting a 'dry-brushing' technique (as will be described shortly) gives one a head start, while the finish can be enhanced with the use of washes. Slight physical distressing, by scraping the surface with a keen scalpel blade or a glass-fibre brush, will partially or completely remove factory-printed detail. It also adds some welcome texture to a plastic shell. After all, timber wagons retain a discernible grain texture, even after several thick coats of paint. Such texture needs to be applied sympathetically, noting the direction of the wood's grain on different areas of the prototype and employing the scraping tool accordingly.

Use a sharp scalpel blade to scrape away the printed characters, moving the blade in the likely direction of the wood grain on each plank.

Abrasive pads and sticks are also useful, adding further texture to the surface. Again, keep strokes in line with the grain direction.

The same goes for the use of abrasives. Work from coarse to medium grades, but don't polish the surface too diligently or the texture will disappear. All debris must be removed, and surfaces cleaned and de-greased thoroughly before work continues.

I invariably opt for acrylic paints for all the tasks outlined in this chapter, but enamels can be employed if preferred. The latter will take longer to dry, of course, which can be frustrating. Who wants to wait for hours between the individual stages, compared to ten to twenty minutes with acrylics? The hand-painted planks will look stark at first, but subsequent washes and further weathering will tone everything down. Two or three separate washes of slightly different shades will be beneficial, and careful manipulation with swabs will remove the excess and create streaking effects. If working on an RTR model, the contrasting textures of the hand-painted planks and the factory finish will be greatly enhanced by the washes.

Allow the final wash to dry completely before refining the weathering with further paint applications or dry pigments. As with most weathering jobs, adopting a layering approach will pay rich dividends. Sketching a probable time-line in advance is a good idea as it can help you to organize your weathering schedule. Taking a run-of-the-mill timber-bodied mineral wagon as an example, we can list the various states that it would go through during a few decades of work:

• Newly built, pristine livery
• Layers of dirt accumulated
• Ad hoc and light maintenance, patch-painted repairs
• More layers of dirt accumulated, but with fresher paint still discernible from the original finish
• Heavier maintenance and repairs, replacement timber planks installed
• More layers of dirt accumulated
• Change of owner, new markings/numbers applied
• More layers of dirt accumulated
• Further maintenance and life-extending repairs, further (unpainted) replacement timber planks installed
• More layers of dirt accumulated

This list is only a rough guide, but it reveals how a gradual build-up of individual weathering layers can tell the story of a typical vehicle's working life.

After cleaning away any debris, pick out individual planks with an approximation of bare timber. LifeColor's Weathered Wood set provides six different shades, designed to be intermixed and layered to create a wide range of timber effects. Dry-brushing in particular will produce authentic grain patterns. The iron strapping can also be touched in.

As well as bare timber, planks in contrasting colours or slightly different livery shades suggest previous repairs and help bring the wagon to life.

BELOW: Allow the paints to dry before applying overall washes. I often use a mix of Dark and Brown washes from the MIG range, built up over several applications.

MIDDLE RIGHT: Wipe away any excess with swabs, keeping all movements in the vertical plane to suggest gravity-induced streaking.

RIGHT: The interiors of open wagons follow a similar path, with an overall, neutral timber base coat applied before introducing a faux grain effect. Use flat brushes and, with only minimal paint on the bristles, draw it along the planks in line with the grain.

Take the time to build up a number of shades, allowing each to dry (ten minutes for acrylics) until a convincing rendition is achieved. Keep brush strokes oriented to the grain pattern.

Touch in any raised strapping or reinforcing brackets before treating the interiors to a mix of washes. Again, wipe away the excess, leaving the darker pigment between the planks.

Underframes benefit from stippling with a mix of paint and dry pigment. Work it around all the fittings, but make sure the wheel treads and axle bearings are kept clean. Here I'm using LifeColor Track Dirt and Weathered Black paints, along with Golan Dark Earth dry pigment.

Powders, applied dry, give wagon interiors a suitably dusty aspect. Choose shades to suit the likely commodities carried, such as darker powders for coal wagons, rusty reds for iron ore, or greys and creams for stone. For general purpose wagons, a variety of dirty browns will suffice.

The same dirt and dust is likely to reach the outside of the vehicle too, especially around the doors, and streaking from the upper edges. With a small flat brush, apply a mix of powders selectively, brushing away the excess.

Powders also enhance the underframe, refining the inevitably patchy appearance of the brushed-on paint and powder mix. Vary the shades to suggest shadows cast by overlapping components, as well as areas of brake dust and rust. Darker patches suggest thicker deposits of muck that has stuck to heavily greased axleboxes, springs and brake gear pivots.

Combining several layers and techniques results in a more authentic-looking weathered appearance. The suggestion of bare timber on the inside and the occasional replacement plank has transformed this Bachmann model.

PLANKED VANS

There are obvious similarities between timber-bodied open wagons and vans. However, while there is seldom an interior to treat, there is a roof to contend with. Any type of planked van benefits greatly from some of the processes already discussed. Picking out individual planks with differing livery shades – and occasionally one in a contrasting colour or left as bare timber – can create extremely lifelike results. Once again, building up the weathering in layers is essential.

These methods are not limited to any particular scale, as all sizes of model can be treated effectively. Indeed, the only necessary change of approach is to employ progressively finer paintbrushes as the models get smaller. Furthermore, modellers in 'N'-gauge can get away with a more impressionistic approach to bare timber, unless you are particularly obsessive.

DRY-BRUSHING

Dry-brushing is a technique that has been around for as long as I can remember. I have no idea where it originated or where I first came across it. I assume my dad passed it on to me as I was

The same processes have been employed with this Oxford Rail mineral wagon. The textured underframe adds a welcome touch, while the patch-painted number panels – themselves weathered with powders – tell the story of an aged wagon that has changed ownership at some point in the past.

These techniques aren't only suited to models in 'OO' and larger scales: these Farish 'N'-gauge wagons have been treated with exactly the same methods.

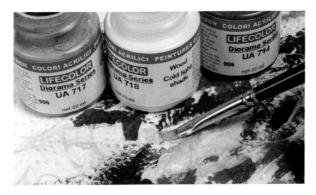

Dry-brushing consists of loading a brush with paint and then wiping virtually all of it on to tissue, leaving only a trace on the bristles. Choosing the right colours is important.

Dry-brushing effects can be tailored by the amount of paint left on the bristles. This cattle wagon is receiving a variety of creamy, off-white shades to mimic the distinctive lime-wash staining of the prototypes. Soft, flat brushes are best, such as this special angled brush from Expo. Apply only light pressure.

When used together with other weathering techniques, in this case washes and powders, dry-brushing offers plenty of potential.

not much of a reader of modelling magazines or books in my youth. Regardless of the background, dry-brushing offers an effective means of highlighting raised detail, such as rivet and bolt heads, iron strapping, door hinges, lamp brackets, and just about anything else that sits proud of the surface. It's also useful for creating other effects, such as smudging and streaking.

It is not always a precise technique, but it can be tailored to achieve different ends, purely by governing the amount of paint that is retained in the brush's bristles. After dipping the brush into the paint, most of the media is wiped away on to a piece of tissue. For very delicate work, such as picking out handrails or subtle relief, virtually all the paint should be removed before the brush is lightly dusted over the model.

Over years of experience, I've found that flat brushes are better suited to dry-brushing, and preferably those fitted with soft bristles – though stiffer brushes also have their uses and can produce their own peculiar effects. Expo Tools recently released an excellent set of angled flat brushes, expressly for dry-brushing. Available in a range of sizes, they do make the job easier and can be worked into awkward areas or up against raised edges more efficiently. Indeed the size of the brush, as well as the shape, is also important. Smaller tools are naturally suited to work over smaller areas or where accuracy is paramount, while larger brushes will cover a wider area more efficiently. More bristles means more fluid retention, so you must be careful to remove most of the paint on to the tissue before dealing with the model.

Dry-brushing is damaging to the bristles, and even the most diligent cleaning can't save the brush from rapidly losing its shape. Therefore I tend to keep a separate collection of brushes for this purpose, usually those that have passed their best for quality painting work, thus giving them a new lease of life in a less demanding role.

Another factor in dry-brushing is the choice of paint. Creating burnished metal effects, on handrails and so forth, is possible using metallic paints. Alternatively, to create subtle highlights on raised details, dry-brushing these in a lighter shade of the underlying colour is highly effective.

We'll see more dry-brushing and similar techniques throughout this book, but it's worth encouraging experimentation from an early stage in order to appreciate how different brushes and paints react on a variety of surfaces. You'll soon learn to judge how much, or how little, paint to leave on the bristles, and to decide which colour to employ.

Both acrylics and enamels are perfectly suited to dry-brushing, although the paint must be shaken and/or stirred to ensure that the pigment is fully dispersed. Viscosity is not too important as we're applying such small amounts, although very thin paint is best avoided. Fast-drying paints, such as Tamiya acrylics, can be dry-brushed, but work must be rapid, and the brushes require cleaning every couple of minutes, so they can be more trouble than benefit.

DOWN BELOW AND UP TOP

The smooth surfaces of plastic and metal underframes, even when 'dirtied' with a variety of paints and dry pigments, can still appear a little flat. Furthermore, vans from the steam and early diesel eras had canvas-covered timber roofs, with a distinctive, textured waterproof covering.

An effective means of replicating texture is to mix paints with dry pigments before applying them to the model. Decant a small amount of paint on to a palette, preferably with a few tonal variations – the livery shade, plus a little black and light grey, for instance – and sprinkle a small amount of dry pigment alongside. Mix the powder and the paint gradually, adding a little thinner if necessary (water for acrylics, white spirit for enamels) until the paint takes on a brushable, yet textured nature. Any brand of weathering powder should be compatible with most paints, but it's best to check application on a scrap surface just in case. Combinations that are known to work well include the paints and powders from the following brands: LifeColor, MIG, Vallejo, Darkstar, Humbrol and Revell.

One factor to bear in mind is that the dry pigments will alter the colour of the paint, so some experimentation will be necessary in order to maintain an appropriate shade. I'm never too particular about the colour of underframes and roofs, as they tend to vary widely between individual vehicles, although dark grey powders are my preferred choice as a roof texturizing agent. Something along the lines of a dark, dirty brown will suffice for underframes. More weathering layers will be added later, so there's no need for things to be perfect at this early stage.

Any form of wood-bodied vehicle can be treated in a similar manner. This brake van is a perfect example, with the various vertical planks being picked out by hand with many variations on the livery shade. A few grey or bare wood planks add even more interest.

A mix of acrylic paint and dry pigment is then brushed over the roof, in lateral strokes, to mimic the textured covering of the real thing. The excess is then wiped gently away with a swab.

The underframe is also treated to a textured coating of paint and pigment.

Washes are then applied to the body, settling into the plank detail. A swab is used to smear the wash over the vestibule windows – these were rarely cleaned in real life.

After allowing the washes to dry overnight, the finish is given a subtle outlook with various shades of dry powder.

The powders will cling readily to the textured surfaces – too readily sometimes, so be prepared to dip a swab in fixative solution to manipulate it if required. Work darker shades around vents, and especially around the stove chimney.

Remember not to blow away excess powder with your breath, but use a broad soft brush to dust it away instead.

AK Interactive's True Metal paints are superb for dry-brushing, imparting a suitably burnished look. The Steel and Iron shades, in particular, are great for handrails and other protrusions likely to receive plenty of wear.

The attention to the planking detail and textured surfaces adds real visual interest to this humble brake van.

Once the textured coating has been mixed, spread it over the roof with a flat brush, working laterally so that any visible brush strokes suggest gravity-led streaking. When dry, the roof can be finished with darker shades of dry powders, brushed around any raised details such as ventilator hoods, gutter strips or, in the case of brake vans, stove chimneys. Again, keep brush strokes in a lateral direction to maintain the illusion that any visible streaks are meant to be there.

For underframes, a smaller brush is required to ensure the textured mix can be worked evenly into all areas. Keep the mix clear of the axle bearings and any electrical contacts or other moving parts, cleaning away any excess promptly. Heavier texture may be desired for a particularly grubby vehicle – add more powder to the mix – stippled around the frames and any bottom discharge chutes that may be present. Once the underframe is dry, the effect can be refined with dry powders, brushed lightly over the surface. Vary the tones to exaggerate shadows and suggest areas of brake dust or rust, as you see fit. You'll find that the powders will adhere keenly to the matt, textured paint underneath, so there will be no need for fixative agents.

FINISHING TOUCHES

Any exposed door hinges, handrails or other metallic protrusions can be picked out with a spot of dry-brushing. Alternatively, running the edge of graphite or artists' coloured pencils across the handrails and other relief, is a viable option. Metallic pencils are also available from art and craft stores, offering a more precise application option. By buffing with a finger or dry swab, some interesting patinas can be produced.

SPATTERING

Spattering sounds as if it might be something that children learn in primary school art classes, but it's a valid technique nonetheless. Basically, it refers to the act of flicking blobs of paint on to a model in order to replicate specific weathering effects. Certain wagon types are more prone to spattering, usually as a result of exposure to dusty commodities in wet weather, such as limestone, china clay or cement. Such materials tend to turn sticky when damp, and the study of prototype images will reveal heavier, textured patches of dirt that contrast with the more generic dusting or streaking effects.

Spattering paint creates a unique effect, especially suited to aggregate wagons. Load a flat brush with paint and wipe away the excess with tissue. Pull the bristles towards you, aim carefully, and then let them spring back, releasing blobs of paint on to the surface.

Again, I prefer to employ acrylics for this technique, loading up a soft, long-haired brush; the bristles are then pulled backwards and quickly released, spattering paint on to the model. It takes a little practice to perfect your aim and judge the quantity of paint that will be emitted, so I would recommend trying out this skill on a scrap wagon or other three-dimensional object.

Some manipulation is possible after the spattering has been applied, using a little white spirit or an acrylic removal agent (such as Lifecolor's), depending on the formula of paint involved. Spattering is never uniform, and once exposure to the elements is taken into account, streaking effects invariably result. Using a swab dipped into the spirit or removal agent, the flecked paint can be dragged vertically to create smudges and streaks as desired. If you're not happy with the results, simply wipe the paint away and start again.

Follow the spattering with some dry-brushing

The spattered acrylic paint can be manipulated with white spirit or remover agent. Use a swab to drag the blobs of paint downwards.

Add more variety in tones and texture by dry-brushing similar shades on to the wagon body, interior and underframe, using prototype images as inspiration.

A further light coat of weathering, using paints and/or dry powders, blends everything together.

and smudging with flat brushes, using a variety of shades, to add further tonal variety and texture to the surface; this will also helping to bring out some of the relief in the wagon's structure.

Be aware that spattering is bound to look unnatural when used in isolation. However, when applied as part of a layered approach, it can be made to look far more harmonious. For best results, apply a generic base coat of weathering, using paints, washes and/or powders before and after the spattering stage. Furthermore, spattering with more than one shade of paint brings even more realism to the picture.

WHAT NEXT?

The techniques suggested here demand very little investment in terms of materials or apparatus, while the amount of time and imagination involved is purely up to you. I suggest practising the various methods on a number of wagons, consolidating your knowledge and enhancing your confidence before embarking on more adventurous tasks. Indeed, in order to take things further, we must start considering the use of an airbrush, which is the subject of the next couple of chapters.

CHAPTER SIX

AIRBRUSHING – THE BASICS

The airbrush is a tool designed to lay ultra-fine layers of paint on to a surface. It has the ability to create a host of unique effects, from the seamless blending of different colours, to the rendering of delicate streaks and misted 'smoke' stains. Some modellers assume that airbrushing is a 'black art' and requires an excessive financial outlay. The latter was once true, but the prevalence of high-quality budget tools and equipment has changed this aspect of the hobby immeasurably. As for it being an impossible trick to master, all you need do is follow a handful of basic rules, and the rest is simply down to practice.

Although the features of individual brands and models of airbrush vary, the same basic principle remains at the heart of the device: the transfer of a liquid medium on to a surface, using compressed air. The air supply must be constant, and the pressure adjustable, so that it can convert the liquid paint into a fine mist.

Airbrushes fall under two main classifications, denoting how the paint and air are mixed together: external and internal mix.

EXTERNAL-MIX AIRBRUSHES

External-mix airbrushes are the cheap tools often offered as a free gift with a magazine subscription or as part of a beginner's painting kit. However, they may as well be packed inside a Christmas cracker, and in my opinion are a complete waste of time and money; they are more accurately described as a mini spray gun than an airbrush.

The paint and the air are mixed outside the tool, hence the 'external mix' moniker. When the trigger is depressed, the compressed air is released and

There are many different types of airbrush: internal and external mix, single and dual action, and with a variety of nozzle sizes to choose from.

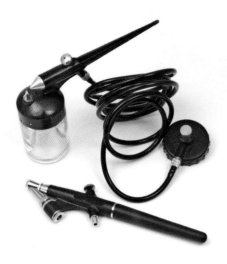

External-mix tools are cheap, but they can be tricky to operate with any level of finesse.

and paint released. This movement is known as the 'action', and airbrushes can be designated as either 'single action' or 'dual action'. With single-action tools, a rotating wheel at the tail end moves the needle fore or aft, decreasing or increasing the paint flow. Making fine adjustments can be fiddly, and the user only has immediate control of one aspect at a time (the trigger controls the airflow only).

By contrast, the trigger of a dual-action airbrush governs both the paint and airflow simultaneously. Depressing the trigger releases the air, while paint is only emitted once the trigger is pulled backwards. The further the trigger is moved, the greater the

passes over a nozzle linked to a paint reservoir. The resultant vacuum draws the liquid into the airstream, and the amount of flow is governed by altering the distance between the nozzle and the air jet. A spanner or thumbwheel is usually provided for this, but making adjustments is not easy – and virtually impossible while the paint is flowing. The coarse, uncontrollable spray pattern is rarely conducive to the art of weathering, although the tools can be easy to dismantle and clean (about the only advantage that I can think of!). While they are very cheap, their unreliable performance probably puts more people off airbrushing for life than offers an affordable route into the hobby.

INTERNAL-MIX AIRBRUSHES

As the name suggests, in an internal-mix tool the paint and air are combined internally, by means of a gravity or siphon-fed paint cup. Paints must be thinned carefully, to a viscosity not much thicker than water. As a result, we can work with lower air pressures and operate close up to the model for greater accuracy.

An adjustable needle sits within the airbrush, and when this is moved back and forth, the gap in the nozzle opens and closes, governing the amount of air

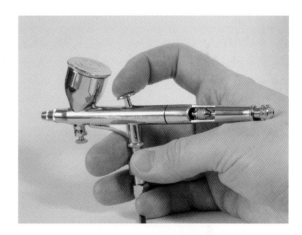

Internal-mix, dual-action airbrushes are recommended for fine weathering work. The trigger governs both the airflow and the paint.

With single-action airbrushes, the paint flow is controlled by a wheel at the tail end. Making fine adjustments whilst spraying is not easy.

paint flow. Offering greater versatility, the dual nature of the trigger takes a little getting used to, but the results can be far superior, especially for detailed work.

NOZZLES AND NEEDLES

The needles of internal-mix airbrushes are machined to match the nozzle's aperture, and any discrepancy will lead to erratic paint flow. Therefore the needle and nozzle can be viewed as the heart of an airbrush, and they must be treated with the utmost care.

In general terms, the size of the nozzle dictates how readily a fluid can pass through it. Consequently, tools with smaller nozzles demand thinner paints and a more rigid cleaning and maintenance routine. It also follows that the fineness of the spray increases as the nozzle size decreases. Most multi-purpose airbrushes have 0.5mm-diameter nozzles, which is fine for general weathering work in 4mm scale and above. However, smaller nozzle sizes, such as 0.3mm, offer a greater level of finesse for more detailed work, especially in 'OO' and smaller scales.

CHOOSING AN AIRBUSH

The airbrush you choose very much depends on the type and frequency of work it is expected to undertake. There is little point spending a fortune on a tool unlikely to see regular use. On the other hand, modellers with exacting standards and who expect to airbrush regularly will be advised to opt for a high-quality tool that can withstand regular cleaning and dismantling. Furthermore, although there are plenty of second-rate airbrushes in the budget sector, there are still some quality ones to be found. I would recommend keeping to recognized brands, such as Sparmax, Iwata, Harder & Steenbeck or Badger. I would also urge you only to buy an airbrush from a reputable dealer, most of whom will offer a warranty and spare-part support. Besides, there are often some great deals to be found for combined kits of airbrush, air supply and accessories.

PAINT CUPS AND NOZZLE RIMS

Siphon feeds rely on suction to mix the paint and air. Intended primarily for overall paint jobs, a minimum amount of paint must be loaded into the siphon for it to work effectively. This leads to wastage, especially as we often employ minimal amounts of paint when weathering. Gravity-feed airbrushes are better suited to small jobs, and the cups may be fixed or interchangeable, sitting on top of, or to the side of the tool. Smaller cups mean less weight in the hand and a better view over the nozzle for greater accuracy.

The shape of the airbrush's nozzle rim affects how well it can operate close to a surface. With ring-type rims there can be a risk of 'blow back', where the air rebounds from the surface, back into the nozzle; this disturbs the flow of paint and makes intricate work difficult. Crown or wing-shaped rims allow the air to dissipate freely, even when the airbrush is pressed against a surface, although the spray pattern is not contained as effectively when working further away. Helpfully, many airbrushes offer a choice of interchangeable rims, either supplied or available as separate accessories.

PRE-SET HANDLES

Fitted to some dual-action airbrushes, pre-set handles consist of an adjustable screw that limits

For weathering in 4mm scale and smaller, an airbrush with a 0.3mm needle/nozzle combination is ideal.

AIRBRUSHING – THE BASICS 53

Pre-set handles limit the movement of the trigger on a dual-action airbrush, governing the amount of paint released.

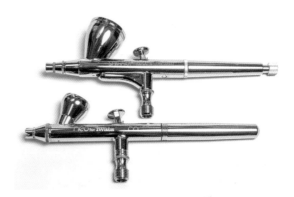

My favourite budget-priced tools: Sparmax MAX-4 and Neo for Iwata CN. Each offers impressive performance and reliability, provided they're well maintained. The MAX-4 even includes a pre-set handle.

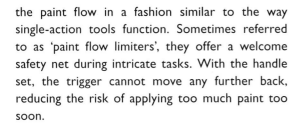

At the lower end of the mid-range bracket, Iwata's Revolution AR, BR and CR are hard to beat. Great value, easy to clean, comfortable and ultra-reliable, the 'no frills' specification keeps cost down without compromising performance. I've been using these intensively for well over a decade!

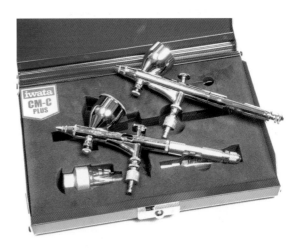

For the serious enthusiast, the Iwata Hi-Line HP-CH and Custom Micron CM-C+ airbrushes have all the extra features necessary for professional work. These are the tools I employ on more precise weathering jobs, in all scales.

the paint flow in a fashion similar to the way single-action tools function. Sometimes referred to as 'paint flow limiters', they offer a welcome safety net during intricate tasks. With the handle set, the trigger cannot move any further back, reducing the risk of applying too much paint too soon.

COMPRESSORS

Electric compressors are by far the most reliable air source, but as the majority of modelling applications require a maximum air pressure of only 20psi (pounds-per-square-inch), some form of pressure regulation is desirable. Indeed, for most weathering

Sparmax produce some excellent low-price compressors that are perfect for weathering work. The ARISM is small, lightweight, quiet and portable. The airflow is smooth and controllable, with a pressure gauge, in-line moisture filter and hose provided. For regular work, investment in a larger unit with an air tank is recommended. Sparmax's TC-610H offers all you'll need in a rugged, reliable and great value package.

Budget-priced compressors can't be expected to cope with working hard on a daily basis, so a more powerful unit may be needed. I've been using an Iwata Power Jet Plus (right) for years, and have found it well up to the work required. The twin-piston motor provides plenty of power, and the handle doubles as the air tank. Recently I have upgraded to a Power Jet Pro, and the encased unit, despite not having an air tank, is quieter and just as able to cope with the demands that I place on it. Each compressor includes a moisture trap, pressure valve, gauge and hose.

tasks, a lower pressure – in the region of 10–12psi – is preferable.

Low air pressure gives the modeller more control over the paint flow, as well as the ability to work more effectively close to the surface. Most modern compressors offer some form of pressure control and gauge as standard. An air tank avoids the need for the compressor's motor to be constantly running, and produces a completely smooth supply of air, free from any 'pulsing' that is a feature of many small, cheap devices.

However, working at low pressures means that an air tank is not essential, and a pressure-regulator valve will iron out any major fluctuations in the airflow.

MOISTURE HAZARD

Compressing air creates heat, and when that air passes through a hose or into a tank it cools, forming condensation. This moisture must be intercepted by a filter, or it will play havoc with the paint. Moisture filters are often supplied with a compressor in the form of a fixed unit, combined with the pressure regulator. Alternatively, in-line filters are cheap accessories that connect between the hose and airbrush, sometimes incorporating a rudimentary pressure regulator valve for fine adjustments.

CLEANING AND MAINTENANCE

I can't stress enough the importance of keeping your airbrush clean and well maintained. Adopting a routine of regular flushing between paint applications will keep the tool at optimum performance. A thorough clean at the end of every session is also recommended. It shouldn't be necessary to strip the tool completely, simply removing the needle should be enough to permit the flushing out of any stubborn deposits.

All decent airbrushes come supplied with instructions for dismantling, cleaning and maintenance. Take the time to study these carefully before use, and keep them to hand for future reference.

The pressure valve, gauge and moisture filter are essential features of a compressor. If they don't come fitted as standard, they are available separately.

In-line moisture filters, such as this Sparmax Silver Bullet, are a cheap alternative to a fixed unit on a compressor. Because I live in a damp part of the world, I employ a moisture trap on the compressor and the air line, just to be sure.

Other vital accessories for airbrush work include glass mixing jars, paint filters (tea strainers are useful), stirrers and pipettes. PTFE tape and an adjustable spanner ensure that the air-line connections are tight and leak free.

A facemask is essential whenever spraying paint, thinners or cleaning fluids. If you intend to airbrush regularly, consider a fume extraction booth to protect your health.

BASIC AIRBRUSHING TECHNIQUES

Mastering the basics of paint flow, spraying distance and air-pressure settings is vital for successful airbrushing. Personally I am happier thinking about just one thing at a time, so I recommend concentrating on a single aspect to begin with, and exploring the other factors in your own time. In addition, before throwing paint at a model, it may be better for the beginner to refine their technique on a more forgiving surface, such as sheets of paper or card, and move on to old toys or scrap models once they feel more confident in what they're doing.

Using pre-thinned paints means there is no need to deal with thinning ratios and viscosity, so we only have the air pressure and the workings of the airbrush to worry about. Ready-to-spray paints are available from Com-Art, Badger and Vallejo (acrylics), as well as the Alclad2 Mil-Spec enamel range.

Pre-thinned water-based paints are ideal practice mediums. They are ready to spray, non-toxic and easy to clean up. Shake the paint thoroughly before loading into the airbrush.

We can strike out one more factor too, by setting the airflow to around 15psi. Indeed, this can be viewed as a default pressure setting for virtually any airbrush weathering job. Veering a few psi either way for specific tasks will help – but let's not get into that just yet.

HANDLING THE AIRBRUSH

A few basic tenets must be remembered from the outset. First, it is vital to keep the airbrush moving whenever the paint is being emitted; dwelling in one place leads to puddles or drips forming. If using a dual-action airbrush, it is important to get into the habit of operating the trigger in the correct order. This will avoid a number of problems, especially spattering at the start and end of every application. With practice and repetition, this soon becomes second nature. The correct operation sequence (and resulting actions) is as follows:

1. Depress the trigger (air on)
2. Move the trigger backwards (the paint begins to flow)
3. Push the trigger forwards (the paint flow ceases)
4. Release the trigger (air off)

Having filled the paint cup with paint, we can turn on the air supply, set the pressure, and aim the nozzle at a sheet of card. Press the trigger and adjust the flow of paint, moving the airbrush in sideways movements. Try and adopt the habit of momentarily releasing the trigger at the end of each stroke, before depressing it again as the airbrush moves in the opposite direction.

Notice how distance plays a role in affecting how the spray pattern appears on the card, and what happens when the airbrush stays still for too long. Drawing lines on to the card and attempting to follow them with the airbrush is an excellent way of improving your aim. Messing with the airflow is also worthwhile, noting how the paint flow becomes coarser as the pressure drops, spitting and spluttering until it stops altogether. Turn up the air pressure and the paint becomes mistier, but it will be harder to control, especially close to the surface.

With the air pressure returned to around 15psi, it should be noticeable that the airbrush is comfortable working at a distance of between 4 and 10cm from the surface, although the paint flow will become more diffuse as the nozzle moves further away. To be able to work effectively at less than 4cm, we may need to drop the air pressure slightly, say to 10–12psi, although the paint may not perform as well at this lower setting, so we may need to thin it slightly. However, if you try working with this thinner paint at a higher air pressure, you're likely to struggle.

Spending a few hours playing with the variables of paint viscosity, air pressure, distance and movement will provide an understanding of each factor. They are interdependent, so it is important to get them all in order so as to achieve the best results from an airbrush.

Devoting time to these basic exercises will also reveal how important it is to clean the airbrush regularly. Note, too, that acrylic paints, due to their fast-drying nature, are more liable to clog up the airbrush unless the tool is flushed through every few minutes. This can be a tedious chore, but if you get into the habit of spraying cleaning fluid through the airbrush at regular intervals, this will keep it working for longer. Filtering the paint before filling the airbrush is also recommended, especially for acrylics.

Begin spraying on to a sheet of card or paper in freeform fashion, just to see what happens. Altering the paint flow, distance and air pressure each has a marked effect on the spray pattern.

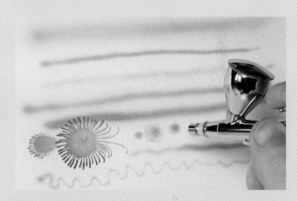

To achieve even coverage, the airbrush needs to be kept moving at a consistent distance from the subject, and the paint built up gradually to avoid runs and puddles. Practise back and forth strokes, working the trigger to start and stop the paint in the correct sequence.

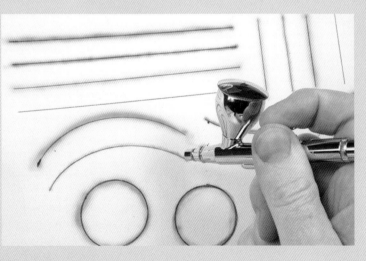

To improve your aim, draw various straight and curved lines and shapes on to the card, and follow them as closely as possible with the airbrush. Work horizontally, vertically and in a circular motion: this is excellent practice for weathering work.

THINNING PAINT

A look at the microscopic gap in an airbrush nozzle through which the paint is expected to flow will reveal just how important paint viscosity is. How can we expect the paint to flow freely unless it is thin enough to enter the nozzle and be atomized evenly by the compressed air?

If the paint is too thick, it will clog up the airbrush's insides or be emitted in a coarse, spattering pattern. We can go too far the other way, though, with overly-thinned paint difficult to control and

Shake or stir the paint thoroughly before pouring it into a mixing jar. Use a pipette to add a few drops of suitable thinner, and stir well.

Keep testing the viscosity by picking up plenty of paint on the 'paddle' end of a stirring tool and watching how it drips. We're aiming for self-contained, round blobs that drip freely, revealing the shiny metal of the stirrer.

the medium's opacity greatly reduced. With thinner paint, we do have the facility of lowering the air pressure considerably until the paint flow becomes more manageable. Indeed, despite the paint being somewhat translucent in this state, this does give us the option of using it for specific effects, such as filtering (see Chapter 18).

As paints differ between brands, I recommend employing the same brand of thinners and paint to ensure complete compatibility. As mentioned in Chapter 2, enamel and acrylic paints must be mixed only with enamel or acrylic thinners, as there is no common solvent suitable for both.

Apart from those already mentioned, virtually all paints require thinning before spraying. No matter what brand or formula, we need to aim for the same viscosity. Ignore stated ratios of paint/thinners, as performance differs enormously according to brand, batch, shelf life, ambient temperatures and goodness knows what else. It is far better to gain an appreciation of the required consistency, and for this, may I present my own scientific method, known as the GD Drip Test!

After shaking and/or stirring the paint in its container, decant an amount into a glass mixing jar, straining it through a filter if you suspect any debris to be present (especially if the rim of the pot is covered in crusty deposits). With a pipette, add a few drops of the appropriate thinner – just a few for now – and begin stirring gently. We're aiming for a consistency slightly thicker than water, similar to skimmed milk. This can be discerned by lifting an amount of paint on the 'paddle' of the stirring tool and watching how the fluid falls away. If the paint clings to the tool or drips slowly in stringy columns, then it's too thick and more thinners can be added.

Continue thinning, a few drops at a time, and stir, checking regularly how the paint drips from the stirrer. Once the paint falls away in round, self-contained blobs, then it is ready. With a polished metal stirrer you should be able to see the shiny surface showing through the paint, with some of the paint's pigment ideally clinging to the bottom edge of the 'paddle'.

If the paint runs off the tool uncontrollably, leaving no traces of pigment behind, then the paint is too thin. Either add a little more paint and try again, or tip away the mix and start from scratch; adding more paint to an overly-thinned mix doesn't always work.

The paint should be used quickly before it has a chance to settle, when paint and thinners will separate. Regular shaking or stirring (every couple of minutes) is recommended if the paint is being used a little at a time. The viscosity should also be checked intermittently, with more thinners added if necessary. Thinned enamels remain workable for an hour or two, but acrylics need using as soon as possible or they start to solidify, which will play havoc with the airbrush.

TROUBLESHOOTING GUIDE

It is inevitable that problems will arise when airbrushing, no matter how long you've been practising. Below is a list of the most common issues and suggested remedies, which should help you to understand where you're going wrong.

Problem: No paint emerging.
Reason/cure:
- Nozzle is blocked – remove needle and nozzle, and clean
- Paint is too thick – empty and clean the airbrush, thin the paint correctly
- Lack of air – check the compressor and airline for leaks, increase pressure
- Breather hole in the paint cup is blocked – clean the lid
- Not enough paint in the cup (siphon-fed tools)

Problem: Paint is emerging but is hard to control.
Reason/cure:
- Needle may be loose – ensure that it's seated fully in the nozzle and that the locking nut is tight
- Needle may be damaged – check and replace if necessary

Problem: Paint is emerging but in a spattering effect.
Reason/cure:
- Air pressure is too low – raise the pressure up to a maximum of 20psi. If it continues to spatter, the paint may need more thinner
- Nozzle is blocked – check and clean
- Needle may be damaged – check and replace if necessary

Problem: No air.
Reason/cure:
- Compressor is faulty, or canned propellant is empty/blocked
- Leaking air – check the hose connections
- Faulty trigger – check the trigger is installed correctly, check the air valve in the airbrush (it may be sticking)

Problem: Rough paint finish.
Reason/cure:
- Air pressure is too high – reduce pressure to 10–18psi. If the paint won't flow, it needs more thinners
- Airbrush is too far from the model's surface – move the airbrush closer, ideally to between 30 and 60cm
- Nozzle may be blocked – check and clean if necessary

Problem: Paint runs off the model and forms wet puddles.
Reason/cure:
- Paint is too thin – either mix a new batch of paint or reduce the air pressure
- Spraying too much paint at once – ease off the paint flow and build up layers very gradually, allowing each to dry
- Airbrush is remaining static while spraying – keep the tool moving

Problem: 'Spider' effect on the surface.
Reason/cure:
- Airbrush is too close to the surface – move it further away

- Paint is too thin – either mix a new batch of paint or reduce the air pressure
- Air pressure is too high – reduce the pressure

Problem: Bubbles in the paint cup when spraying
Reason/cure:
- Nozzle is blocked – dismantle and clean
- Needle may be loose – check and tighten the locking nut

At regular intervals (every five minutes with acrylics, fifteen minutes with enamels), or when switching between colours, pour out excess paint from the airbrush and flush the tool with a suitable cleaning fluid. Wipe the inside of the paint cup with tissue and a cotton swab. This cleaning pot from Sparmax contains a filter to trap noxious fumes and waste fluids.

Cleaning fluids are available to suit different types of paint. Stronger solvents, such as Liquid Reamer and cellulose thinners, will shift anything, even dried paint, but they must be handled with care. Check whether your airbrush has solvent-proof seals before opting for strong cleaners.

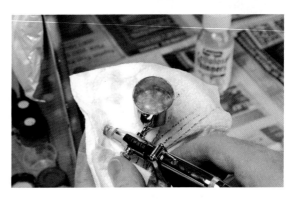

ABOVE: At the end of a painting session, repeat the flushing stage. After a couple of flushes, fill the cup with more cleaning fluid and cover the nozzle with tissue. Ensure that the air pressure is not set too high (a maximum of 15psi), and press the trigger. The air will be blown back into the cup, along with any traces of paint. Tip out the dirty fluid and repeat until the fluid remains clear. Be sure to wear eye protection!

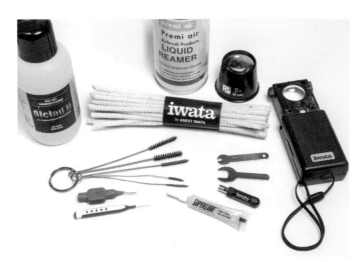

LEFT: Cleaning kits make the job of airbrush care easy. Small pipe cleaners and brushes will keep the tool's insides spotless. Your airbrush should be supplied with a nozzle wrench and instructions for cleaning and maintenance.

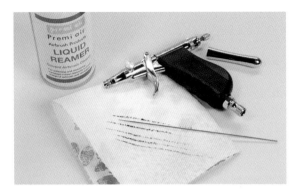

Carefully remove the needle from the rear of the airbrush and wipe it on tissue dampened with cleaning solution. Spray air through the airbrush while the needle is removed to clear any residues.

Apply a drop of lubricating gel to the needle, a centimetre or so from the tip, before sliding it gently back into the airbrush. Check that it is seated in the nozzle correctly, then re-tighten the locking nut. Repeating this quick routine at regular intervals will avoid many potential problems, while also removing the need for dismantling.

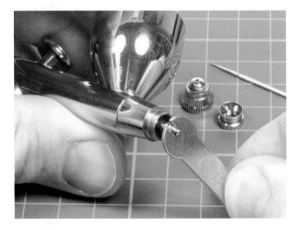

If the airbrush does become clogged or the needle sticks, remove the nozzle cap and, with the supplied wrench, gently unscrew the nozzle itself. This should free a stuck needle, which can then be removed from the tail end.

Fill a jar with cleaning fluid such as Liquid Reamer or cellulose thinners, and drop in the smaller parts to soak. This is where a good quality airbrush, with solvent-proof seals, will repay the extra cost.

RIGHT: **Add cleaning fluid into the airbrush and insert a brush at the nozzle end to clear any debris from the inner surfaces, wiping the bristles after each pass. Don't force large brushes into the airbrush or the needle packing seals will be damaged. Repeat until the brush comes out clean. Re-fit the nozzle with the wrench, to finger tightness only (or the thread will be stripped), lubricate and replace the needle, then test by spraying cleaning fluid through the airbrush.**

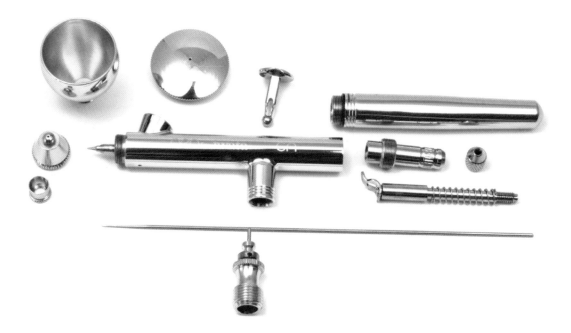

A *full strip-down and service should only be necessary very occasionally, provided the tool is cleaned and lubricated at regular intervals. Follow the supplied instructions carefully, and lubricate the air valve, trigger and needle during reassembly. If in doubt, contact your local dealer and have it professionally serviced.*

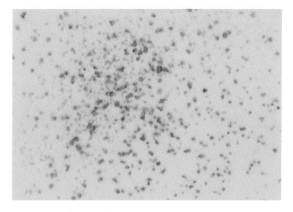

If the airbrush produces a spatter pattern, it is likely that the paint is too thick or the air pressure is set too low. Alternatively, the nozzle may be blocked or the needle damaged.

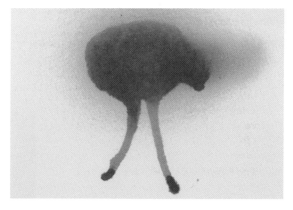

The airbrush must be kept moving while paint is flowing, otherwise runs and puddles are created. The risk of puddles increases when the paint is thinned excessively.

CHAPTER SEVEN

AIRBRUSHING IN PRACTICE

Having dealt with the basics of airbrush operation, we can now put the device to good use. A handful of projects is suggested here, designed to help improve control of the airbrush, most notably in terms of mastering the paint flow and precise application. These tasks will also foster an understanding of how the air-pressure level and distance, from the airbrush to the subject, affects how the paint behaves.

Tank wagons are one of my favourite teaching aids. The cylindrical barrel, convex ends, complex underframe, and impediments such as walkways, ladders and filler hatches, offer a wide variety of challenges to the airbrush user. It is therefore recommended that you obtain a fleet of cheap, second-hand or budget-priced tank wagons as practice aids: these will provide a great platform on which to hone your technique.

THE LIMITATIONS OF AIRBRUSHES

Great as airbrushes can be, they do have their limitations, and to rely solely on these devices for an

Start with a simple wagon and mix up a suitable weathering shade, thinning as necessary. With the air pressure set to around 15psi and the airbrush about 4–5cm from the surface, begin spraying a very fine mist. Keep a scrap of card on hand to test the paint flow before pointing the airbrush at the model.

When happy, move on to the model, keeping the paint flow set to a minimum to retain control. Remember to keep the airbrush moving at all times, in horizontal and vertical strokes.

RIGHT: Manoeuvre the airbrush and rotate the model on a turntable to allow the paint to land on all the various surfaces and contours. Keeping paint flow to a minimum may make for slow progress, but it allows the 'dirt' to be built up evenly over the whole model.

entire weathering job may not always be the best option. A good example is a timber-bodied wagon: getting the 'dirt' into the narrow recesses between planks with an airbrush is very difficult, regardless of the model's scale. The last thing we want is for bright, clean patches of paintwork to be visible within recessed areas, as these are the places that will be the filthiest on the real thing!

One of the ways around this issue is to spray the whole body in the 'dirt' shade, ensuring that it sits on all faces of the moulded relief by moving the model and the airbrush to ensure paint approaches from every possible angle. Then, as we did in Chapter 5, employ cotton swabs and a little solvent to wipe paint away from the faces of the planks, leaving dirt in the recesses. This can be a labour-intensive process, and often may not justify the use of an airbrush, when washes or hand-applied paints can do the job more efficiently. Indeed, what I aim to show over the next few pages is that combining manual and airbrush techniques, and different weathering media, offers superior results.

Airbrushes do have their limitations. This 'O'-gauge van looks good at first glance, but closer inspection reveals that there is no dirt in between the planks. A preliminary application of a weathering wash would have been more successful.

This 'HO'-scale van has been treated to an overall 'brush-on, wipe-off' treatment, using a mix of LifeColor acrylics. The airbrush then adds finesse to the finish.

The roof has been treated in similar fashion, with all strokes from the cotton swabs running laterally to create authentic streaking. The airbrush then moves in the same directions, exaggerating the shading around the ribs and softening the overall effect. Heavier deposits of dirt are concentrated towards each end of the roof.

TACTICS FOR WEATHERING TANK WAGONS

My tactics for weathering tank wagons typifies my usual approach to many rolling stock projects. The application of washes is an optional preliminary step, dictated by the nature of the prototype and the desired final appearance. Older style, riveted barrels greatly benefit from the use of washes, but this may not be necessary on smooth, modern tank barrels, unless a particularly streaky effect is required.

As we have seen, washes offer the benefit of concentrating controlled amounts of 'muck' around raised and recessed detail, and in this instance, that means the saddle area and any fillers, hatches and walkways attached to the barrel. The underframe and particularly the solebars may also benefit. The translucence of most washes means that they will struggle to modify a predominantly black colour scheme, and will therefore need help from regular paint formulas. Washes also offer contrasting sheens to the matt paints usually sprayed through an airbrush, or the dusty nature of weathering powders. With vehicles carrying oils and liquid fuels, some greasy-looking streaks will be essential.

Such areas of relief will be difficult to treat with an airbrush alone, though not impossible. Tank access walkways and ladders can act as stencils as the airborne paint passes through the gaps, creating a strange shadow effect on the surfaces behind. Unless the paint is sprayed from multiple angles, or a form of mask applied behind the fixtures, this often results in the wagon emerging far dirtier than you may have originally intended.

The combination of manually applied and airbrushed media makes for a far more convincing end result.

Here, the airbrush is creating 'dirt' deposits around the raised detail and softening the harsh appearance of the individually painted planks. With correctly thinned paint and a low air pressure (10–15psi), we can work up close to the surface for optimum accuracy.

Care is needed to ensure even coverage across the chassis, moving the airbrush around all the underframe detail. The airbrush also works to blend in the stark white decals, applied over the partially weathered sides.

Another area where the nature of the model poses a challenge to the airbrush is when working paint into enclosed spaces. The air that carries the paint from the airbrush has to disperse somewhere, and with no way out of a confined space it is likely to bounce back towards the tool's nozzle. This 'blow-back' effect makes control of the paint difficult and may result in a messy, spider-like effect on the surface.

We can work around this issue, to a point, by lowering the air pressure to around 10psi, although the paint must be thinned correctly in order to flow freely at this reduced pressure. Alas, thinner paint is more likely to misbehave and run off the surface unless applied in ultra-thin layers, creating something of a balancing act for the airbrush user. Working with an airbrush fitted with a crown- or wing-shaped nozzle cap will help, by allowing the air to disperse more readily. We can also remove the outer nozzle cap completely, if desired, for very close-up spraying at low pressures. However, this places the delicate tip of the needle at risk of damage, so great care is needed.

If parts likely to cause problems for the airbrush can be unclipped and safely removed, so much the better: preliminary weathering can then take place on the various components separately, before they are reassembled and blended with further weathering work. However, in order to hone your skills with washes, paints and the airbrush, try and work with these parts in situ.

WEATHERING PROCEDURE FOR RTR WAGONS

If water-based acrylic paints are to be employed on an RTR wagon, a preparatory coat of matt varnish is sprayed over the whole body and underframe, unless enamel washes are to be applied in the first instance, which will provide a suitable intermediate coating on which the acrylics can grip successfully. In most cases I shall be working with RailMatch enamels, and work begins with Frame Dirt, worked into the underframe and wheels. The model and the airbrush are kept moving to ensure that all faces of the intricate relief are treated to an even coverage. Either hold the inverted model in a gloved hand or mount it in a padded cradle device, leaving the chassis fully accessible. Also, if you'll be using tension lock or other NEM couplers, keep them installed at this stage as they should also be weathered.

THE UNDERFRAME

Add a little Roof Dirt to the previous colour to darken it slightly and to add more tonal variety to the chassis. Work this darker shade into the deeper recesses to exaggerate the shadows, or pick out areas likely to be greased, such as pivot points and suspension fittings. Introduce a dash of Dark Rust into the mix and attempt to pick out the brake shoes.

By reverting to the original Frame Dirt, these contrasting shades can be toned down if desired, blending everything together until the chassis elements appear coherent, but not one-dimensional. It takes time to get things looking exactly how you want them, although with repetition, we can soon speed things up. Remember, if you realize that too much weathering paint has been applied, use a cotton swab dipped in white spirit to remove the excess. Once the solvent has evaporated, we can start again.

Tank wagons offer a wide range of challenges. Why not invest in a selection of budget or secondhand models on which to practise?

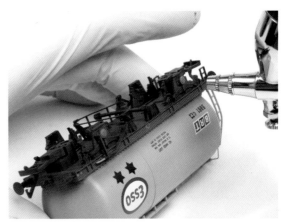

TOP LEFT: **With many wagon projects, I begin by removing the wheels and treating them to a coating of general weathering shades, either by hand or airbrush. A mix of Tamiya acrylics has been employed here before the tyre faces and flanges are cleaned thoroughly.**

TOP RIGHT: **The underframe is treated next, with the model held upturned in a gloved hand. An initial spray of RailMatch enamel Frame Dirt is being applied, working it round the complex moulded detail. Keep paint flow to a minimum to avoid overdoing things, which can happen quickly.**

Add extra tonal variety by mixing in a little RailMatch Roof Dirt, followed by Dark Rust to mimic brake dust.

When switching between different shades in the airbrush, particularly if going from a dark shade to a lighter colour, it's a good idea to flush the tool quickly with a little cleaning fluid. It need only take a moment or two, but it will help keep the tool working at its optimum level and reduce the risk of annoying blockages and spattering.

THE BARREL

Once the underframe is satisfactory, the model can be mounted on a turntable and attention turned to the barrel. Using the Frame Dirt shade once again, the paint is aimed along the lower edge of the barrel, working horizontally initially. The angle of attack is varied to ensure that the paint reaches into the saddle. This is where you'll appreciate the benefits of mounting the model on a raised turntable, as the airbrush will have to be angled from above and below.

Paint flow must be minimal at all times to maintain full control of how much 'dirt' is being applied. Bear in mind that this is only the first of several layers that the wagon will receive. Furthermore, limiting the paint also guards against the risk of creating runs of excess liquid on the surface.

Light, vertical streaks can now be introduced, working from the top downwards and following any seam lines. Aim to keep the airbrush nozzle at a consistent distance from the surface, even as the tool follows the curvature of the barrel. This is easier said than done, but it's an important skill to learn. Remember that if the airbrush moves further away, the spray pattern will be wider and more diffuse, while if it gets closer, the paint will create a narrow, more defined streak.

With the underframe treated, mount the model on a wood block secured to a turntable to allow for unhindered access from all angles. Start adding RailMatch Frame Dirt along the lower edges of the barrel, followed by gentle vertical strokes to pick out any pronounced seams.

The airbrush must be aimed from different angles so that paint can find its way into recessed areas, especially around (and beneath) the tank top walkway and filler hatch. Repeated passes are essential, keeping paint flow to a minimum.

With a mix of RailMatch Frame Dirt and Roof Dirt, more vertical streaking is introduced, aiming to keep the nozzle at a consistent distance, in sympathy with the curvature of the barrel. Narrow, defined streaks require the airbrush to be up close. Wider, diffused streaks are created from further away. Keep the paint flow limited to a delicate mist.

Describe circular arcs with the airbrush to work the paint round the end profile of the barrel, followed by vertical streaks.

Going darker still, with Roof Dirt alone, the process can be repeated. This time, concentrate the paint into the deeper recesses and immediately around the raised detail, especially the filler hatch and the top of the walkway, to enhance the shading effect. More streaks and shading can then be added to the barrel, concentrating on the upper two-thirds. I tend to follow a rule of thumb where the weathering is 'browner lower down', as this tends to be how real rolling stock appears.

Moving to a darker shade – a mix of Frame Dirt and Roof Dirt – the tricky task of aiming the paint under and around the filler hatch and walkway follows. Again, patience and minimal paint flow are essential, attacking the subject from all angles to ensure even coverage.

Mix in darker shades, such as Weathered Black, to create even more tonal variety. Add darker shading beneath the walkway and hatch if desired.

For heavy staining, add a touch of RailMatch Matt Black to the Roof Dirt/Weathered Black mix, and layer more streaks and shading. Dwell slightly with the airbrush aimed around the filler hatch. After a split second, start moving the airbrush downwards, tapering off the paint flow as you go.

When working on the barrel ends, move the airbrush in a circular motion to deposit a misting of paint around the edges of the model's profile. You'll need a degree of flexibility in your wrist, but this is a very useful practice exercise for promoting freer movement while spraying.

More concentrated streaking can now be added, with the addition of Matt Black to the mix. Streaks may peter out before the bottom of the barrel, and this can be achieved by gradually reducing paint flow while the airbrush moves in its downward trajectory.

A little gloss varnish can add some welcome greasy texture and suggest more recent spillage, but the clear coat is best applied once the weathering paints have dried fully.

Some variety can be added by wiping away the paint from number panels and safety instructions using a swab dipped in white spirit, followed by a light misting of more paint from the airbrush to blend these areas back into the overall picture.

It's important to ensure a degree of variety amongst similar wagons. Cleaning away paint from number panels or safety legends and differing the degree of staining will avoid uniformity.

FINISHING TOUCHES

After an overnight rest, the wheels can be refitted and the finishing touches added, such as scuffing and burnishing to the ladders and walkways, using the dry-brushing technique or coloured pencils. Also, greasy deposits around the axleboxes, discharge pipes and brake-gear linkages can be touched in by hand using washes or paints.

Study plenty of prototype images to see how specific tank wagons tended to weather: some may have been kept relatively clean, while others could be filthy.

An alternative approach is to start the process with weathering washes. Layer brown and dark washes, allowing each coat to dry. Use swabs to wipe away the excess and create subtle streaking effects.

Washes are especially useful for 'N'-gauge tanks, especially those with plenty of surface relief.

Once the washes have dried, the airbrush can refine the effects and add extra streaking and shading effects.

It helps if strapping and ladders can be temporarily removed while the airbrush is being employed, allowing it clear access to the barrel.

A swab dipped in white spirit will clean away enamel or fresh acrylic paints from around number panels and other important legends.

THE BENEFITS OF PRACTICE

In this chapter we have seen how effective a tool the airbrush can be, especially when combined with manual techniques. However, practice is required in order to master the various factors, especially concerning the preparation of paint, adjusting airflow and the physical control of the tool. But devoting the time to hone the fundamentals of airbrush weathering will be repaid with superior results and a more enjoyable experience. Practising on numerous examples of the same wagon type allows you to concentrate on the processes without worrying about devising specific approaches to different vehicles.

We must bear in mind, however, that uniformity of weathering is something we ought to avoid. Certainly similar wagon types tend to incur similar weathering patterns, especially those working together for long periods. But it's rare that more than one or two wagons will have exactly the same amount of dirt and grime, nor will the deposits be in exactly the same place, so some variety is called for.

As the following chapters will show, an airbrush offers a great deal to the weathering effect, but it's certainly not a tool that can do everything.

The barrel strapping has now been refitted and the airbrush is gently misting over the cleaner areas to help blend everything together.

The use of washes at the outset ensures pigment is retained in those awkward pockets and recesses, while the airbrush adds a refined touch.

CHAPTER EIGHT

TURNING TO DUST: CEMENT AND SCRAP WAGONS

Certain freight commodities leave an indelible mark on the rolling stock employed to carry them. This chapter takes a couple of popular cargoes – cement and scrap metal – and offers a number of ways of recreating the distinctive weathering patterns associated with the real vehicles. As well as capturing the right shades of 'dirt', we also need to harness the appropriate textures. Cement is a very dusty material, and when exposed to moisture it becomes sticky and lumpy, so this facet needs to be emulated in miniature.

Scrap-carrying wagons have always received rough treatment at loading and disposal facilities, seldom being cleaned unless during a major overhaul. As well as accumulating thick layers of filth, steel-bodied wagons are prone to distortion and corrosion. We can copy these features in a number of ways.

TANKS WITH TEXTURE

Tank wagons for powdered goods, such as cement, industrial sand and chemicals, demand a slightly different weathering approach to those outlined in the previous chapter. While the basics of weathering with an airbrush apply, the differences lie in the choice of paint shades, the nature of streaking effects, and especially in the range of textures. By way of example, a handful of PCA cement tanks is featured here, with the initial weathering stages the same as those of the oil tankers seen previously. A preliminary coat of clear, matt varnish was applied to give a flat, dusty sheen and to provide plenty of 'grip' for layers of dry pigments.

After the generic 'dirty' colours had been airbrushed (RailMatch Frame Dirt, Roof Dirt and Weathered Black), paler greys were added to the

With this PCA cement tank, the initial weathering stages followed a similar approach to the oil tanks in the previous chapter. A variety of grey-brown shades followed, to better suit the prototype's dusty cargo. Plenty of fine streaks were created by operating the airbrush in close proximity to the surface, following the barrel's profile as the nozzle moved downwards.

An initial coat of matt varnish ensures that the dry pigments cling effectively to the surface. Using a small flat brush, a variety of grey powders was carefully applied, concentrating heavier deposits around the filler hatches.

While the airbrush offers the chance to create subtle streaking effects, the essential dusty, grainy texture can only be recreated with dry pigments.

mix, and as with the prototypes, a greater number of fine streaks were rendered along each side and end.

The airbrush has to be much closer to the surface to achieve these fine lines. However, keeping the nozzle at a consistent distance from the curved barrel takes practice.

Once the painting stage was complete and the wagon thoroughly dry, powders were applied, enhancing the streaks created by the airbrush. The dead matt surface allows the powders to cling tenaciously to the barrel, and heavier deposits of dry pigment were stippled around the filler hatches. The dusty, grainy texture is typical of the prototype, and plenty of variety is recommended between individual vehicles.

The iconic BR Presflo cement hopper, as modelled in 'OO' by Bachmann. They would rarely appear pristine, so weathering is essential.

IMPRESSIVE PRESFLOS

The BR-designed Presflo bulk powder carrier is another wagon type that provides an ideal basis for honing one's airbrushing skills. The complex nature of the vehicle's profile makes it difficult to spray paint consistently around all the horizontal and vertical ribbing. Employing the same three RailMatch enamel shades as the tank wagons in the previous chapter – Frame Dirt, Roof Dirt and Weathered Black – work begins with the wheels and chassis. Moving upwards, the body is treated next. The model must be moved around, preferably on a turntable, and the airbrush pointed at various angles to allow the paint to attack the complex profile. If the results appear excessively dirty, employ swabs and

Weathering a Presflo with an airbrush can be a challenge, but it is worth persevering. Offering an excellent platform on which to practise paint control and precision application, it is essential to approach the model from all angles.

white spirit to remove the excess, but leave the 'dirt' in the many recesses.

The walkway and filler hatches on top of the hopper pose a challenge, but can be treated in a similar manner to the tank wagons in Chapter 7. Once happy with the paint coverage, the wagon will need an overnight rest to dry out completely.

The matt weathering paints provide the perfect surface to which weathering powders can adhere, and a variety of greys and dark browns can be mixed together on a palette. The dry pigment is stippled on to the surface, starting around the filling hatches and working downwards over each side and end. The motion of the brush should mimic the direction of how the cement dust would streak downhill in reality, with the excess swept away with a soft brush.

Keep varying the shade of the powder mix to avoid an overly uniform appearance, building up a number of layers until the desired effect is achieved. Add heavier deposits to the upper face of the chassis, working the pigment round the vacuum cylinders and down on to the chassis. A few drops of Tamiya acrylic thinners from a pipette will help secure the pigment. When dry, further layers can be added and the process repeated, creating wonderfully crusty deposits.

To seal the rest of the pigment, a fixative solution can be misted over the whole model using an airbrush. Reduce the air pressure to the minimum

Begin to work the pigment down the sides of the hopper and on to the underframe. Vary the mix to introduce tonal variation, adding more of the Europe Dry Mud shade. Use the edge of the brush to create narrow streaks, and allow the pigment to settle on any horizontal surfaces.

With a flat brush, work a mix of pigments around the filler hatches and over the sloping hopper top, keeping brush strokes in line with how gravity would cause streaking on the real thing. I'm using LifeColor PG105 Dry Dust, PG106 Damp Dust, PG117 Ash and PG116 Europe Dry Mud, plus a smidgeon of MIG P039 Industrial City Dust. A stippling action will help the pigment cling to the matt surface.

Treat the ends in a similar fashion, working the pigment around the brake gear and other fittings.

To secure heavy deposits of pigment, drop a small amount of fixative solution, or Tamiya acrylic thinners, on to the surface with a pipette. Allow it to permeate the powder.

Once dry, further pigments can be stippled or lightly brushed on to the surface, depending on the required texture. The process can be repeated indefinitely until the desired effect is achieved.

Fixative can also be sprayed through the airbrush, using a low air pressure to avoid blowing away the pigment. Only a light misting is needed.

The crusty outlook created by the pigments looks wholly appropriate.

setting at which the liquid can be sprayed satisfactorily, and apply a light layer from a distance of about six to eight inches away. As the fixative lands, the model will appear slightly cleaner, so be prepared to add further layers of powder after about ten minutes, and more fixative if necessary.

Once satisfied with the overall effect, set the model aside for a few hours to dry. Although the finish should prove resilient, we need to take care when handling the model in future, lest any pigment be worn away.

Thanks to the use of fixative, the heavily weathered finish is resilient enough to be handled.

SCRAP WAGONS

Over the years, scrap metal has been transported in all manner of open wagons. Regular loading and discharging by mechanical or magnetic grabs, in the filthy surroundings of scrap terminals and steelworks, led to these wagons taking on an air of dereliction that mirrored that of their cargo. The modern air-braked POA/SSA wagons introduced in the 1980s are a prime example, looking knocked about and careworn within a couple of years of entering service.

Shown here is a sample approach to recreating a typical fleet of steel-bodied scrap carriers, using a mix of washes and powders. Building on the techniques we've already mentioned, the process is taken further, with layers of washes stippled to create a more tangible texture, followed by heavy powder applications. Fixative solution is employed to manipulate and partially remove the dry pigment, allowing further, lighter layers to be applied. In turn, these are physically manipulated with stiff-bristled brushes.

In fact, these scrap wagons have been treated without any recourse to an airbrush, reaffirming what is possible using manual techniques alone. I'm not sure what more the airbrush could have brought to this project, other than being the means of applying the clear matt varnish prior to the pigment applications, or maybe adding some finesse to the final weathering, especially of the chassis.

It's not only scrap wagons that can be treated in this way: the techniques can be used happily on many other steel-bodied freight vehicles working in similarly harsh conditions.

From this point, dry pigments will be used, so a suitably flat finish is essential. Revell's matt clear coat, in aerosol form, is an excellent surface primer for powders. Allow it to dry overnight.

Enamel washes can create all sorts of effects, depending on how they're applied. Pieces of natural sponge, dipped into the wash, will create a more nuanced stippling effect. A mix of MIG's Dark and Rust Effects washes produces a believable corroded texture when built up over several layers.

BOTTOM RIGHT: A mix of three pigment shades – LifeColor PG101 Golan Dark Earth, PG107 Eroded Burned Rust and MIG P236 Grimy Black – is dappled on to the surface, and worked into all the ribs and underframe details. Aggressive use of the brush will destroy the bristles, so use a cheap brush or one near the end of its life.

Mix up a darker shade, adding more of the MIG Grimy Black, and work this into the corners of the panels and into any deeper recesses.

Sweep away the excess powder with a clean but stiff brush, using vertical strokes. Raised surfaces will take on a welcome, burnished appearance, but don't worry about perfecting the finish just yet.

Dip a swab in pigment fixative and work it into the body panels to manipulate the powders and clean them away from number and instruction panels. The random 'rust' effect of the sponge-applied washes will also be revealed, having been protected by the intermediate layer of varnish. Keep the swabs away from the edges of the panels to maintain the heavy deposits of muck here.

Once the surface dries out, further pigment layers can be applied gently with a soft brush. This will minimize any hard edges created with the fixative and swabs.

Repeat the process on each side and the ends, followed by the interior. If a permanent load is to be installed, we need only treat the upper few millimetres.

Some wonderful textures can be created, and the partially revealed number panels are an authentic touch.

A more restrained approach is planned for this wagon. Lighter coats of MIG Brown and Dark washes are applied, and as they begin to dry, a flat brush introduces pronounced streaking effects.

As before, matt varnish has been applied with an airbrush, followed by gentle application of the same shades of powders, using a soft brush. A stiffer brush then burnishes the surface with downward strokes.

The burnishing action picks out the edges of the ribs and other fine detail, especially around the underframe. More of the initial washes are visible, offering a welcome contrast to the earlier, blue version.

REALISTIC SCRAP LOADS

Scrap-metal loads can be recreated using all manner of waste material, but I prefer to stick with plastic components that can be bonded together quickly and easily. Anything from spare kit components to sprue material and offcuts of plastic sheet or strip will do, along with the swarf created when cutting or drilling. Chopped into small random chunks, the conglomeration can be piled on to a sheet of thick plastic card, cut to create a false bottom and to be a snug fit in the wagon's interior.

Secure the scrap with plenty of liquid poly cement (work in a well-ventilated area – it will get very smelly), applied using a pipette or syringe in a similar manner to ballasting track. The solvent will penetrate the pile and cure to a solid mass after a few days. If the load is to be permanent the scrap can be secured in situ, but for removable loads, a suitable wooden jig is required. This will contain the piled cargo on the former during bonding, yet will prevent the material from sticking to the sides. Once bonded, the load and its former can be removed from the jig and placed into the wagon.

After priming and painting with a variety of dark reddish-brown and grey shades, the relief can be treated to a light brushing with various brighter shades of 'rust'. Finish by dry-brushing with metallic shades, such as gunmetal or iron, to give the individual components a metallic 'edge'. Dry powders can also be applied sparingly, to add some welcome dusty, gritty texture.

Scrap wagon loads can be created cheaply and effectively using chopped-up plastic waste. After priming, an overall coating of various red-brown and grey shades is applied by hand, followed by successive dark wash coats.

Using a variety of 'rust' shades of LifeColor acrylic, mixed with a little dry pigment for added texture, brush these lightly over the scrap to pick out the relief and create plenty of tonal variety.

Dry-brushing with high quality metallic paints, such as AK Interactive's True Metal range, will really bring the scrap load to life. For best results, use a few different shades, such as iron, steel and gunmetal.

These scrap loads are incredibly cheap and easy to create, making use of otherwise waste materials.

CHAPTER NINE

RUST IN PEACE: PART ONE

The creation of realistic rust deposits must surely be one of the main aspirations for modellers, especially where freight rolling stock is concerned. As well as a coating of general grime and dust, steel-bodied freight wagons have always been prone to corrosion, especially in the pre-1990s era, before the adoption of more rigorous maintenance regimes and better quality paint finishes. Certain ready-to-run models have been offered with factory-applied rust and corrosion effects, although this is usually limited to a spray of red-brown paint. Occasionally this can look effective, especially when viewed from a distance – indeed, some of Bachmann's and Dapol's recent factory-weathered output has been rather impressive. However, real corrosion is seldom a single shade of brown, and many subtle tonal and textural shifts are visible.

Recreating rust is possible in numerous ways. Some intriguing, innovative products have appeared recently, ranging from rust-coloured, textured paints to tiny metallic particles that can be painted on and chemically corroded. Some of these concoctions are better than others, excelling in different situations or in particular scales. Throughout the next three chapters a range of techniques will be outlined, growing steadily in complexity, but all

being readily achievable with the minimum of fancy tools, equipment, time or financial outlay.

In this first instalment we'll keep things simple, using only paints, washes and dry pigments, while the use of an airbrush will be kept to a minimum.

LAYING THE FOUNDATIONS

Creating surface texture with abrasives helps ordinary paint to replicate the distinctive gritty appearance of corroded metal. Furthermore, we know that paints, washes and powders will cling more effectively to a rough surface, thus providing greater scope for creating a variety of streaking and smudging effects. With RTR stock, any printed logos and legends will need to be distressed, along with the surrounding paintwork. With kit-built models, we'll need to distress the transfers to prevent them looking too pristine (see Chapter 19); alternatively it may be preferable to apply the lettering by hand with an ink pen.

Suggesting areas of ad hoc repair work can be highly effective and prototypical. It has always been important for railway staff to be able to identify individual revenue-earning vehicles, so reinstating numbers and weight markings was common practice during maintenance. The simplest solution was to quickly apply a panel of fresh paint – usually black – before adding new markings on top. As usual, researching prototype images will throw up all manner of fascinating individual examples as inspiration for your own projects.

GETTING TO WORK

Texturizing the surface is a simple process, employing a range of abrasive sheets, pads and sticks of coarse and medium grades. Working round raised details and complex profiles can be tricky, but

The standard of factory-weathered RTR models has definitely improved, with some adventurous rusty versions appearing in recent years. The tampo-printed corrosion on this Bachmann hopper is impressive – although we can do much better!

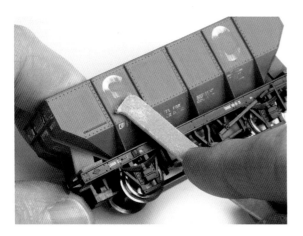

Create surface texture and add a suitably distressed outlook with abrasives. Keep all the strokes vertical, and remove as much of the printed detail as desired.

Clean away the debris and apply a preliminary wash coat. Here, a mix of Dark and Brown MIG washes has been brushed on and the excess wiped away. The textured surface will retain plenty of the pigment.

strokes should be kept vertical wherever possible, to suggest the effects of the weather. Work lightly, with minimal pressure on the abrasives, remembering that the aim is to distress rather than remove the existing finish. Cleaning away the dust is important, though we need not do this as assiduously as if we were aiming for a flawless finish. A brush-over with an alcohol-based cleaner is sufficient, followed by a wipe with cotton swabs to lift off the debris. A couple of applications will also ensure that any greasy deposits from our hands have been removed.

Once dry, a preliminary application of weathering washes will start the texturizing process. It's at this point that you will appreciate the need for maintaining vertical strokes with the abrasives in the preliminary stages, as the washes pick out the undulations in the surface, creating some wonderfully subtle streaks, helped by the use of swabs during application.

GOING RUSTY

The initial wash coats will need an overnight rest to dry completely before we can start creating the actual corrosion. There are plenty of suitable paints available these days, from many different brands and across various formulas. As usual with my work, I tend to employ a mix-and-match approach, although I do prefer acrylic paints for much of my 'rust' creation jobs: the fast-drying nature of acrylics allows them to be overlaid rapidly, which can be crucial when building up a wide range of shades and tones. Employing a variety of brushes, swabs and natural sponge adds to the variety of textures and creates more random patterns of 'corrosion'.

Consider where the heavier deposits of rust are likely to appear on your vehicle; research prototype images if necessary. In general, rust appears where the paintwork is more susceptible to damage or where water is likely to be trapped, such as in the bottom of open wagons or within recesses. Riveted joints and panel seams are also inevitable weak points.

Start with the worst affected areas, as these will need more layers of paint. Rust never appears as a single shade, but shows up as a wealth of yellow/orange tones at one end of the spectrum (usually signifying the freshest corrosion) to reds and browns at the other. I tend to start with the darker shades, patiently stippling the paint in small quantities and moving gradually towards the lighter shades.

LifeColor's broad range of rust tones is a real boon in this respect. It is possible to work with only a handful of paints, of course, mixing them together

Starting with the darker shades of LifeColor's 'Rust Wizard' liquid pigment set, the heavier deposits of corrosion are being added around the edges of each riveted panel.

The thin liquid pigments can be built up over several layers to suggest thicker, coarser rust deposits, while stippling lighter shades with a piece of natural sponge will create more random patches.

After building up the desired amount of rust using a variety of shades, the effect can then be toned down with an application of general weathering tones, using powders, washes or an airbrush. A mix of Tamiya acrylics is being used in this case. Note the new number and weight legends, applied with an ink pen over black panels.

The interior of wagons can be dealt with in similar fashion, with paints and washes employed to build up a dirty, corroded outlook. However, bear in mind that certain wagon interiors will be stained by the commodity, so this coal hopper is being treated with a dark mix of dry powders.

The layered approach has culminated in an attractive model.

on a palette to create a broad tonal range, but simply shaking and opening eight or ten pots of ready-made shades makes the job easier, particularly for the busy professional. Indeed, as I was writing this chapter, LifeColor released some new 'liquid pigment' packs, one of which is aimed at rust effects. These are something of a cross between regular acrylic paints and washes, offering some unique performance characteristics – one of the most useful is that the tone and texture of each colour differs according to how many layers are applied.

One of my favourite materials is Modelmates' Rust Effects. This medium offers a wide range of shades and textures, with dark and crusty deposits achieved simply by applying several layers. Furthermore, both LifeColor's liquid pigments and Modelmates' Rust Effects can also be applied sparingly for some incredibly subtle, almost translucent effects.

Whatever medium is employed, rust patches and streaks will look effective on top of the preliminary weathering washes. However, we should also weather the rust, to help it blend in with the surroundings, and to suggest that the corrosion has been ongoing for some time, rather than suddenly appearing. Further washes are an option, but the rust may need sealing first; for example, the Modelmates dyes remain permanently water soluble, so a coat of varnish is essential before any other medium is applied. Powders and/or the use of an airbrush and paints will finish things off nicely.

As regards powders, dry pigments can also be used to create rust deposits, with virtually all ranges offering a few suitable shades. Stippled on to a matt surface with a fine brush and manipulated with fine swabs and a little fixative solution, delicate streaking and smudging effects are also possible. However, powders can look a little flat when used on their own, but by applying them over a base of wet paint, or indeed, by mixing them with paints before application, some interesting textures can be created. Open wagon interiors are where the powder and paint mixture comes into its own, because such areas are crying out for a greater amount of gritty, rusty texture.

I am an enthusiastic user of Modelmates' Rust Effects. After distressing, this wagon is receiving several layers of the medium, creating crusty textures and a broad range of tones.

As usual, the heavier deposits of corrosion are concentrated around the edges of panels and doors, while a sponge adds a random array of smaller patches.

After airbrushing with a mix of Tamiya acrylics, the overall effect is impressive. Don't forget to seal Modelmates dyes with a coat of varnish.

Another wagon treated with Modelmates Rust Effects, applied by brush and sponge, and complemented with airbrushed acrylics. The texture of the simulated corrosion is subtle but appreciable.

The hopper interior has been treated in a similar fashion, but with heavier layers of the Rust Effects to suggest larger areas of bare, corroded steel. Dark, dry pigments produce a suitably dusty environment.

Regular paints can also be effective in the simulation of rust. Choose a range of shades, such as this trio of LifeColor acrylics, to add tonal variety. Again, start with the darker shades, before layering and blending other tones with a fine brush.

Although the painted splotches look a little crude to begin with, once refined by misted general weathering from the airbrush or dry powders the results can be acceptable. The more restrained texture lends this technique to 'N' gauge.

Dry powders are especially effective when used in conjunction with washes. The various rusty streaks and patches on this wagon, for example, offer something a little different.

Further variation in rust tones and texture can be obtained by using enamel washes alone. Rust-coloured formulas do exist, but they can be complemented by the reliable combination of MIG Brown and Dark washes, applied with a stippling action. For a grittier finish, store your washes upside down, then dip the brush into the gloopy deposits left in the lid. Dabbing the wet surface with swabs also adds extra texture.

AIRBRUSHED RUST

The use of a good-quality airbrush, with a fine needle and nozzle combination (0.3mm or smaller), optimally thinned paint and – most importantly – a steady hand, can be combined to create realistic rust patches. A few years ago while testing a new Iwata Custom Micron airbrush, I devised extreme challenges to see how good the tool was in terms of precision and control. As a result, I realized that I could create almost pin-prick-sized rust patches on freight wagons in scales down to 'N' gauge. Furthermore, by gently moving the airbrush's nozzle in vertical strokes, and tailing off the paint flow at the same time, some wonderfully authentic streaks were created. Further realism was added by overlaying a couple of different rust shades.

The 'full stop' technique, where the airbrush is used to create tiny dots of paint, is an excellent way to perfect our control of the air and paint flow, as well as developing the confidence to work right up close to a surface. Practising on a sheet of card, with a series of dots drawn in rows, helps to perfect your

After applying the corrosion and general weathering effects, don't forget to add further visual interest with a little dry-brushing. Humbrol's enamel Gunmetal (No. 53) is ideal, and Expo's special angled flat brushes make application easier.

eye–nozzle co-ordination. After an hour or so, you should feel confident enough to work on a model. Indeed, this is an exercise that I encourage students on my airbrushing courses to try for themselves, as it also helps them to keep the tool steady and to appreciate the range of delicate effects that a good airbrush is capable of.

For the adventurous, the airbrush can be employed to add rust deposits. Press and slowly move the trigger backwards to emit a tiny flow of paint, cutting off the flow once the paint has built up sufficiently (usually after one or two seconds). Practise by drawing a series of dots on a piece of card to improve your aim and control of the paint flow. Gentle vertical strokes, tapering off the paint as you move, will create effective streaks.

Spend time practising before trying your skills on a model. The distance between nozzle and surface will dictate the size and opacity of the patches, and varying the paint shade slightly will make for more realistic effects.

Airbrushed rust patches appear different to hand-applied corrosion, but no less convincing. Indeed, it is good practice to introduce plenty of variety to your wagon fleets.

Airbrushing rust is easier on larger scale subjects, and with further practice we can build up layers of paint over the same patch in order to add a degree of texture. Good control of the paint flow is essential to avoid puddling or runs.

As well as faint streaks created by the airbrush, we can enhance our rust patches with the use of paints or washes.

Remember that keeping the airbrush still while paint is being emitted will eventually lead to a puddle of paint forming, but being able to toggle the trigger back and forth (on a double-action airbrush) without moving the tool is a useful skill to master, as will be seen in later chapters. An airbrush fitted with a paint flow limiter, or 'pre-set handle', will prove invaluable for such tasks.

CAN WE DO BETTER?

We've talked about the importance of layering, and this is especially valid with reference to cor-rosion. Although the results achieved thus far can be judged as realistic, the fact remains that in this recreation process the rust is appear-ing on top of the paintwork instead of beneath it. The following chapter addresses this issue, which is not as difficult to resolve as you might think.

The vivid rust stains can be toned down with a light brushing of dry powders.

While these techniques can be effective, the rust is still on the outside of the paintwork, which is contrary to reality.

CHAPTER TEN

RUST IN PEACE: PART TWO

The techniques covered in the previous chapter can be effective, especially after a little practice. But this next selection of projects is more ambitious, and employs a more refined approach in the search for ever greater realism. We'll also look into approaching the weathering process much earlier in the finishing process. In fact, for the creation of lifelike corrosion, it's often best to start the weathering before the livery has been applied, rather than after.

FROM THE INSIDE

A handful of rudimentary techniques exists to help us recreate the authentic nature of rusty surfaces, where corrosion is peeling and bubbling from under the paintwork. Liquid masking is the main facilitator of this approach, although I've seen modellers use all manner of other strange materials for the same purpose. Salt and even Marmite have been recommended to me in the past, but to my mind they involve too much mess to be attractive alternatives. My preferred approach also allows greater flexibility in the effects that we can create: anything is possible, from small self-contained rust patches to an entirely corroded bodyshell with few traces of paintwork left intact. Although it looks fiddly, it

ABOVE LEFT: **Mix up a range of rust-coloured shades on a palette, combining them with dry pigment to add a suitably gritty texture.**

ABOVE RIGHT: **Brush on the mixture with a flat brush, employing a stippling action to maximize surface texture.**

LEFT: **Once the base layer is dry, stipple further shades to create lighter and darker tones.**

can actually be effected quickly, and some amazingly realistic effects can be created easily.

The process starts with a primed surface, in the case of an assembled kit, or an RTR factory finish. In the latter case, any printed characters will have to be flattened with abrasives beforehand, or they're likely to show through the rust, which will look very peculiar. A mix of dry pigment and paint is then applied over the entire body, introducing a gritty texture. By building up several layers, using a stippling action and plenty of tonal variation, we can create an approximation of corrosion. How much we do depends on the envisaged final outcome, so for less extreme cases use a modest amount of dry pigment for the initial coats and regular paint to add various highlights and shading. With heavily corroded wagons, add more pigment to the paint for a coarser texture. Be aware, though, that such a heavy approach is likely to obscure much of the fine relief on the model's surface, which may or may not be desired.

Once again I prefer acrylics in these instances, their workability and capacity to dry rapidly giving them a vital edge over enamels. But before we can proceed to the masking stage the paints must be completely dry, which demands a good twelve hours, even for acrylics. Choice of masking fluid is not important, although brands tend to behave in slightly different ways. Less viscous fluids, such as Vallejo's Liquid Mask and Wilder's Quick Mask, can create subtle peeling effects, while Humbrol's Maskol and Phoenix Paints' latex-based versions are thicker and great for more severe corrosion effects. Apply the fluid by brush, cocktail stick or, for more random patterns, a tuft of natural sponge. Don't forget to check prototype images to ascertain which areas of a vehicle are most susceptible to different levels of corrosion.

Once the fluid has dried to a flexible, non-sticky film, the livery coats can be applied by hand, airbrush, or even aerosol if you prefer. The type of paint is not important for this technique, as long as it's compatible with the masking fluid and underlying acrylic or enamel 'rust' layer. In an effort to reduce

the amount of weathering needed later, I like to mix a few different shades of the livery colour, introducing darker areas around recesses, with lighter shades in the centre of panels or over raised areas. This can be done both with the airbrush and by hand brushing.

Once the livery has dried out, a stiff brush is employed to loosen and remove the masking fluid. If you're careful, it may be possible to leave areas of blistered or peeling paint here and there. Sweep away all the loose debris before adding the necessary numbers and markings according to the prototype. If waterslide decals are involved, a few coats of gloss varnish will be necessary before and after application, finishing with a matt clear coat to reinstate the desired flat sheen. Then the final weathering touches of dirt, grime, oil and whatever else is required, can be applied using paints, washes or powders, according to taste.

As for the wagon's interior, all that is required is to apply the initial stages of the textured 'rust', keeping it free from the livery paint and finishing with a general application of dirty paints or powders at the end.

With the corroded finish completely dry, apply masking fluid in targeted areas with a small brush. Alternatively, for more widespread peeling effects, apply random patches by dabbing with a scrap of natural sponge. Leave the fluid to dry to a flexible film.

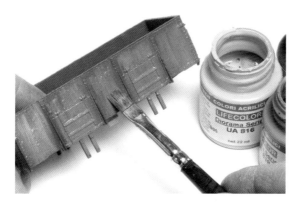

The acrylic livery colours can be applied by hand, with a flat, soft-bristled brush. Introduce tonal variety by adding light grey and black to the livery, mixing the wet paints on the model's surface. Finish with vertical strokes, creating subtle streaks of the different shades.

Leave the paint to dry before employing a stiff, dry brush to loosen and remove the masking film, revealing the corrosion beneath. Note how the different livery shades give the paintwork a lived-in aspect.

After adding number panels and other markings in a suitably distressed fashion, final weathering brings a cohesion to the body and chassis.

Interiors can be left in the all-over corroded finish, duly weathered with paints and powders.

Careful final weathering is important to soften any hard edges and create a more believable model.

The combination of a realistic surface texture and the rust visibly appearing from beneath the paintwork produces a superior finish.

CHIPPING

Railway modellers probably associate the term 'chipping' with the installation of DCC decoders, but in many other disciplines it is a well-known method of creating realistic flaking or worn paint effects. Chipping involves using a temporary masking medium, and allows patches of corrosion, primer coats, or even previous colour schemes to show through the uppermost livery colour. Although similar in principle to the aforementioned techniques, the difference lies in the subtlety of effects that can be achieved.

Acrylic-based chipping formulas, such as those in the AK Interactive range, are clear, odourless fluids that are designed to be sprayed on to a surface using an airbrush. Different 'grades' of chipping fluids exist, with AK Interactive's 'Worn Effects' offering subtle results (see Chapter 11), while the 'Heavy Chipping' version is intended for more pronounced peeling effects.

A few golden rules need to be followed for successful chipping. First, the underlying paint must be completely dry. Any water-soluble finishes, such as Modelmates' Rust Effects, will have to be sealed with a few coats of clear matt varnish before continuing. A number of light coats of the chipping solution must be sprayed on, with most formulas stating a minimum of three layers, allowing each to dry naturally in between (for ten minutes or so).

There is no need to thin the fluids before airbrushing, but due to their slightly gloopy nature they are likely to spatter on to the surface, which is exactly what we want. Set the air pressure to around 15psi. After application, the airbrush can be flushed out with water or a non-solvent cleaning solution. While chipping fluids can also be applied by brush, the results are seldom as satisfying.

When the final layer is dry, the top coat of paint can be applied, again preferably by means of an airbrush. Painting manually is possible, but we risk disturbing the masking medium with the brush. We *must* use a water-based acrylic, such as LifeColor, Vallejo or Revell, rather than Tamiya, and definitely not enamels. Apply a flat coat of the desired shade, as you would normally, or, as with the earlier technique, add slightly lighter and darker shades to create some tonal variety and to minimize the need for weathering later.

Allow the paint to dry for a few hours, then take a clean brush, dip it in water, and begin brushing over the surface in vertical strokes. Soon the water will dissolve the chipping solution, revealing the underlying finish. As much or as little can be revealed as you wish; the process can be halted by allowing the

An alternative to traditional masking fluid is the product known as 'Heavy Chipping', from AK Interactive. Applied by means of an airbrush, several light coats are required.

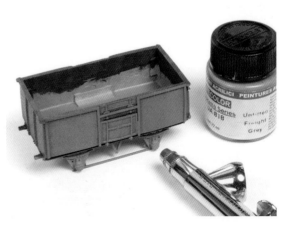

The topcoats can then be sprayed, using only water-based acrylics. Try varying the livery tones, adding highlights and shading.

Allow the livery to dry before activating the chipping solution with water and a clean brush. The amount of chipping can be controlled according to how much water and pressure is applied. As soon as you're happy with the effect, allow the surface to dry naturally.

The process can be repeated, applying different livery colours, or further shades of the same scheme to mimic repaints and a longer history of corrosion and distress. Using a stiffer brush to activate the chipping medium creates a different array of effects.

Add more dry pigment to the base coat and stipple away the chipping solution with a stiffer brush to create heavier texture.

Persuading decals to adhere to such a gritty surface is not easy. In these cases, I opt for a fine Rotring pen filled with white ink. The diagonal stripe was added with a fine brush and acrylic paint.

Misted layers of Tamiya acrylics from the airbrush finish the job. The array of textures and tones is striking.

surface to dry out, something that's not possible with Maskol or other, thicker masking fluids, which must be removed entirely after painting.

A vast range of different effects can be created by employing stiff or soft brushes, sponges, swabs or scouring pads to manipulate the masking layer. If you feel that too much of the top coat has been removed, simply allow the surface to dry out, apply more chipping fluid, followed by the livery, and try again. Several layers can be laid on top of the corroded base coat, to tell the story of a long-lived vehicle, with numerous older paint schemes showing through the battered and worn finish. We can perhaps start with a coat of red primer, followed by an older livery colour or two, before the latest paint scheme is applied. Each individual stage needs to be treated with the chipping fluid, to allow the rust and previous paintwork to show through, before repeating the process as many times as you like.

As soon as the desired finish is obtained, allow the model to dry out before adding any necessary decals and final weathering. A sealing coat of matt varnish will protect the chipping work, although this is not something I usually bother with. Indeed, after further weathering with powders or the airbrush, the finish is usually resilient enough to withstand handling.

ENDLESS VARIETY

One of the best outcomes from both of the techniques outlined here is the fact that it's virtually impossible to end up with two wagons looking identical, due to the random nature of the processes involved. The possibilities for experimentation are endless, and while it may take a few attempts to understand how the various masking and chipping fluids behave, amazingly lifelike effects can be created. The chipping technique does benefit from the use of an airbrush, but the 'Maskol' version is fine for those who prefer to work by hand.

While the work featured here has centred on the bodyshells, the same processes are equally applicable to roofs and underframes. Furthermore, not only are they suitable for steel-built stock, but they are excellent for virtually any vehicle, allowing previous liveries, bare timber and other materials to show through. Indeed, they are so vital and enjoyable that I have begun employing them on coaching stock and locomotives when I consider them appropriate.

CHAPTER ELEVEN

RUST IN PEACE: PART THREE

To complete our trilogy of corrosion techniques, this final instalment looks into how we can alter the actual fabric of the model before any paint is applied. Kits and RTR models rendered in plastic are prime targets for distressing. As well as creating the all-important texture of corroded metal, we can also distort the material to mimic the inevitable results of an intensive working life in a harsh environment. Prototype study reveals where the damage is most likely to occur on specific wagons. For example, the bodywork of open wagons is likely to be knocked about from the loading of heavy commodities such as stone or minerals.

CHEMICAL WORKS

Liquid poly adhesive offers an alternative means of creating surface texture on a plastic model. The thin liquid softens the plastic to a point where a stippling action from a brush will leave a discernible texture. Allowed to harden overnight, the plastic can then be painted and weathered as normal. With factory-applied finishes the solvent will behave in a similar fashion, although any printed characters and logos will disappear beneath the liquefied paint. But again, once re-hardened, the surface will revert to a stable footing.

Highly effective on plastic models in any scale, this is yet another method that is worth experimenting with. I find it especially effective for roughening up the interiors of steel-bodied open wagons, as well as adding texture to the exterior, because the amount of solvent and the means of application can be tailored precisely. A few words of caution, however: first, be careful not to leave inadvertent fingerprints in the softened surface during handling. Also be careful to avoid obliterating fine surface detail, such as rivet heads, door hinges and panel seams. Allow plenty of time for the solvent to evaporate and for the plastic to harden completely before applying paint. The surface is likely to take on a glossy sheen, so acrylic paints may have difficulty in adhering; a light coat of primer may therefore be necessary.

Finally, there is no avoiding the smell of the solvent, and it is essential to work in a well-ventilated area.

Liquid poly cement is designed to soften plastic, so it can be used to add texture to wagon bodywork. Stipple the thin liquid on to the surface using a stiff-bristled brush to create a rougher texture.

Allow the solvent to evaporate completely before priming. Build up a base coat of all-over corrosion, using a variety of shades.

Humbrol Maskol has been employed here as a random masking medium beneath the grey topcoats. Once the film has been removed, the corrosion reveals itself.

Liquid poly cement offers a more refined approach to creating a textured surface, perfect for 2mm scale models

USING A HAMMER AND PUNCH

Using a hammer and punch may seem a crude approach to weathering, but they are perfect for recreating bulging, distorted body panels, particularly those of neglected mineral or aggregate wagons. This method is best suited to plastic wagon kits, preferably before assembly. It can also be adapted to etched brass components, modifying their pristine, flat outlook. I've also had some success with RTR stock, although the thicker plastic offers more resistance.

A flat-headed engineer's punch transfers the impact of the hammer, targeting the distortion more accurately and introducing bulges not dissimilar to the weight of tons of coal or other unyielding materials being thrown into the wagon's interior. Work with the components laid flat on a surface with a little 'give' in it, such as a rubber cutting mat or a cork floor tile. Lay the outer face downwards and pummel the inside with the hammer and punch, using light pressure to begin with, while you get an idea of how the plastic is behaving. Move the punch around the areas to be treated, such as the panels between strengthening ribs, where the bodywork is liable to swell outwards.

Inevitably the blows will cause the plastic to curl upwards, but the parts can be straightened by sub-merging them in hot (not boiling) water for a few moments and then gently re-shaping them. Clamp them as flat as possible while the plastic cools, though of course some of the distortion must be retained. Assembly of the parts may have to differ slightly from the kit's instructions, with the corner joints reinforced from the inside with lengths of plastic angle. Priority lies with getting the chassis frames and axles absolutely square to ensure reliable running.

Taking a hammer and flat-headed punch to plastic kit components, before assembly, offers the chance to create some spectacular distortion effects.

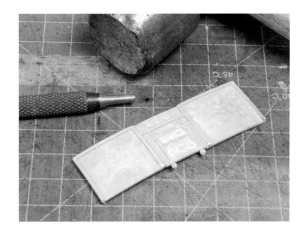

By pummelling the body sides and ends from the inside, a bulging effect is created, reminiscent of years of loading with tons of hard material.

During assembly, the corner joints will probably need reinforcing with plastic angle. To even out some of the physical distressing, a coat of liquid poly produces a more coherent texture.

MAKING ADJUSTMENTS

If the distressing work looks unsatisfactory from the outside, don't worry, as we can address it after the body has been assembled, either with abrasives or by applying liquid poly adhesive to create a more universal surface texture. The upper edges of the body can also be roughed up with pliers or the hammer and punch to add some extra character.

Another option is to apply a coat or two of Mr Surfacer (Grade 500 or 1,000). This lacquer-based primer-cum-filler can be applied by brush, or thinned and sprayed through the airbrush. Adding a subtle surface texture, Mr Surfacer also fills any hairline gaps and provides a perfect base on which to apply paint. Two coats are recommended, abrading the first layer lightly once dry (after an hour or so). Some room for manipulation exists: by applying the second coat with a stippling action, we can introduce a more pronounced texture, as well as minimizing any visible brush strokes.

Whatever physical distressing is employed, this groundwork will stand us in good stead as the weathering and finishing stages progress. Using it in conjunction with chipping and peeling paint techniques will bring an extra dimension to our work.

Mr Surfacer, from Gunze Sangyo, is a combination of filler and primer that can be used with, or instead of, liquid poly to introduce a subtle surface texture. A few minutes after application, as the finish turns tacky, try stippling the surface with a clean brush to create a rougher texture.

Hairspray provides an alternative masking medium. After a base coat of 'corrosion', the wagon is covered in a light misting coat of extra-hold hairspray. The grey livery coats then follow.

After about ten minutes, a stiff brush is dipped in water and used to soften the hairspray, thus revealing the rust beneath.

After adding number panels and markings, only a modicum of final airbrush weathering is needed to finish the job.

The combination of physical distressing before assembly, texturizing with Mr Surfacer, and the hairspray/rust techniques makes for a very realistic 4mm-scale model.

The same techniques have been employed on this wagon, before the unique qualities of LifeColor's Rust Wizard Liquid Pigment set is used to create more tonal variety. Applied by brush and swab in the same manner as washes, the pigments create the look of fresh rust streaking over the peeling paintwork and corroded metal.

Subsequently toned down by an airbrushed mix of general weathering shades, the extra rust layers look even more convincing.

This mineral wagon kit was also subjected to physical distressing before assembly. The harder edges created by the use of Maskol during the 'rusting' phase creates a more pronounced peeling effect.

A greater level of physical intervention is possible on larger scale models. This 7mm-scale kit has been treated with the hammer and punch before the hammer's ball is used to create further bulging of the body sides.

The battered body looks rather rough and ready, but having been braced at the corners with plastic angle it has dried to a very rugged assembly. Care was taken to get the chassis absolutely square to ensure perfect running performance.

The larger scale needs more texture, so a few coats of Mr Surfacer were employed as a primer, the second coat being stippled with a flat brush. A mix of paint and plenty of dry pigment created the overall, heavily corroded finish, before a few coats of hairspray formed the medium for the chipping stage.

Only a few light coats of the acrylic livery colour were airbrushed, with little effort to add high- and lowlights.

Before the paint had fully dried (about five minutes), the surface was worked with a damp brush and a heavy dabbing action, creating some unique effects.

More dabbing of the surface with tissue and swabs added more texture and tonal variations.

Once fully dry, a coat of clear matt varnish sealed the finish, before final weathering with Tamiya acrylics.

Not allowing the grey paint to dry before activating the hairspray has generated an array of streaking and smudging effects.

The slightly bulging nature of the wagon body is clear in this view, a subtle but effective way of adding greater levels of realism.

The various weathering stages have created lifelike texture and tonal variety.

CHAPTER TWELVE

TIMBER WORKS

This chapter considers the particular weathering characteristics of timber-bodied railway wagons. By employing the previously showcased chipping and peeling methods, we can allow bare timbers to show through the paintwork. We can also create three-dimensional wood-grain effects by physically distressing the surface of plastic models.

We touched on the creation of bare timber effects using paint alone, in Chapter 5. A variety of tones should be chosen, aiming to match the character of the materials used on the real thing. Hardwoods and softwoods differ in appearance and weather-ing characteristics, some sporting a greater array of knots or a more pronounced grain figure. There also remains the limitations of the flat surface, be it metal, plastic or resin. The latter two materials can be enhanced freely, the surfaces yielding readily to scribing and scraping tools.

As with the steel-bodied minerals in the previous chapter, working on kit components before assembly makes life easier, but it's not essential. Indeed, it is possible to achieve some stunning effects on RTR stock too, especially in 4mm and 7mm scales.

ABOVE RIGHT: **After a light misting of LifeColor's acrylic, a damp brush activates the Worn Effects solution. Brush strokes are being kept vertical as much as possible.**

ABOVE LEFT: **The chipping process can be just as effective on timber-bodied stock. After some rudimentary airbrush work on the bodywork, several coats of AK Interactive's Worn Effects have been applied.**

LEFT: **To speed up work on the chassis, the body has been masked loosely with post-it notes while the frames receive a dirty mix of weathered black and brown Tamiya acrylics.**

After the model has dried out, the finish can be refined with dark washes to the plank seams, applied with a fine brush directly into the recesses.

Enhance the exposed metal fittings with rust-coloured washes, creating subtle streaks.

New numbers have been applied with a Rotring pen and white ink.

Although the representation of bare timber is fairly basic, the effect is nonetheless appealing, bringing out the best of this Coopercraft plastic kit.

CREATING WOOD GRAIN

Creating wood-grain relief demands a sharp, fine-tipped scribing tool, a steel-wire brush and plenty of patience. I find it best to scribe one or two separate areas at a time, whenever I get a spare half hour or so between other jobs. Attempting to treat an entire wagon in one go, or a small fleet of similar vehicles, can be extremely boring!

Pay attention to the direction of the grain on each component, scribing the plastic accordingly. In general, open wagons and some general-purpose vans feature horizontal planking, with the grain running likewise. In contrast, brake vans feature vertically oriented planks. Vehicles with wooden headstocks will have the end grain exposed on each side, but otherwise the ends of timbers are usually protected beneath strengthening plates of steel or iron.

Deepening seam lines between planks using a profile cutting tool creates extra definition, adding to the sense of depth. Profile cutters form a consistent trench-like cut and must be drawn towards the user to retain full control over the blade. Work against a straightedge and don't cut too deeply, lest the plastic parts are weakened or distorted. Clean away loose debris and add further, finer grain texture with a small wire brush, again working along

For even greater realism, try scribing wood-grain detail into the plastic with a sharp scriber. It helps to work on kit components before assembly.

A profile cutter, such as this Olfa tool, cuts consistent troughs, which is ideal for enhancing plank seams. Always draw the tool towards you, guided by a steel straightedge if necessary.

For open wagons, treat the interior, too. A greater degree of distressing is possible by working a steel wire brush along the direction of the grain. Experiment by softening the plastic beforehand with liquid poly.

Clean up the debris and tidy the joint edges before assembling the kit.

the correct direction of each plank. For very rough timber, such as interior boarding, apply a coat of liquid poly adhesive to the surface, and after a few minutes, run the wire brush over the softened plastic.

I seldom resort to liquid poly for work on the outside of a wagon, for fear of compromising the delicate strapping and bolt-head detail. It is recommended to practise beforehand on scrap models or materials, allowing each process to be tailored to your own tastes. In my opinion this texturizing work actually makes the painting stages significantly

easier, as the recessed grain patterns and deeper seams are more receptive to the use of washes, retaining pigment more readily. Furthermore, the extra surface relief makes dry-brushing work far more effective.

FILTERS

Filters are similar to weathering washes, adding translucent hints to a coloured background. When several different filters are layered, applied by hand or airbrush, some interesting visual effects are pro-

After priming, shades from LifeColor's Weathered Wood paint set were applied. After a few overall coats of generic timber shades, contrasting grain patterns can be hinted at with a little dry-brushing.

When the paints had dried, AK Interactive Light and Brown wood filters were applied, followed by their Wash for Wood. The dark wash sits in the panel seams and the scribed grain detail.

The metal fittings were touched in with rust shades before a few layers of Heavy Chipping medium were sprayed on, prior to the grey livery coats.

To activate the chipping medium, a stiff-bristled brush, dipped in water, was employed.

Once the chipping work was complete and the model thoroughly dry, the surfaces were refined with further enamel washes, working into the recesses and around raised details.

Once the exterior work is complete, the interior can be finished off, with a similar round of filter and wash layers.

duced. AK Interactive's wood-grain filters are an excellent example, creating subtle tonal shifts to the base colours in a much more sympathetic manner than is possible with regular paints. Apply the filters in a number of light layers, allowing them to dry in between coats. Most filters are enamel based, designed to sit on top of acrylics without disturbing them (once they're dry). However, that means longer drying times, of at least a few hours, so it can be a slow process.

Following the filters with dark washes will bring the individual planks and other items of surface relief into greater contrast. When the washes have dried out, the rest of the weathering can begin in earnest, picking out any rusty steelwork if necessary, before the chipping and peeling techniques.

A whole raft of possible effects is possible, from blistering, peeling paint (using masking fluid) to a subtler, worn outlook using AK Interactive's Worn Effects or hairspray as a masking medium.

An unfortunate result of the scribing and texturizing steps is the difficulty that waterslide and rub-down transfers will have in adhering to the surface. A possible remedy involves keeping areas destined for transfers smooth and untouched by the scriber and wire brush. Alternatively, these areas can be flattened and filled where necessary after the texture work has been carried out. Or you can avoid decals altogether, and use paint or an ink pen to add slightly haphazard markings, which often suit a decrepit vehicle better than perfectly executed numbers and letters.

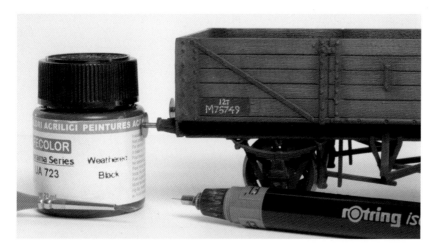

The Rotring ink pen takes care of the lettering and numbering, as decals will struggle to adhere to the distressed surfaces.

After such an involved process, you'd expect some impressive results. This Parkside Dundas plastic kit has been greatly enhanced by the various distressing and painting phases.

A mix of wood-grain and corrosion textures really bring the wagon's surface to life.

There is plenty of tonal variety in the heavily distressed interior.

Although the scribing and texturizing steps are easier on larger-scale models, the same techniques have been used to good effect on this much improved Dapol 'OO'-gauge wagon.

Reflecting a life of hard work, the scribed grain detail and eroded grey livery give this wagon a lifelike appearance.

CHAPTER THIRTEEN

SHADY TECHNIQUES

The technique of pre-shading has the potential to create subtle nuances of tone, and when combined with colour modulation the effects can be highly realistic. As with all practical endeavours, pre-shading and colour modulation can be as easy or as difficult as you want them to be. They offer many benefits, with pre-shading also acting as a dual-purpose primer/undercoat, but both methods allow the creation of high-fidelity finishes and are deceptively simple.

It should be stressed that the following processes are relevant only to airbrush users. Acrylic and enamel paints are equally suitable, and low air-pressure settings (10–15psi) are essential. While you don't have to be an expert with the airbrush, it's important to be able to work comfortably at close quarters and maintain full control over paint flow. Subtlety and patient application are the keys to success.

PRE-SHADING BASICS

So, what is pre-shading? It is a technique that consists of applying the darker 'shading' elements of a weathered finish before the livery has been painted, and is quite a drastic departure from the orthodox approach of starting with a fully finished, pristine model. At its most basic, pre-shading can begin with a model undercoated entirely in black. The prototype livery is then sprayed on top, without allowing the paint to settle within recesses or up against raised details, as would usually be the norm. Several ultra-light coats are required to build up the colour, keeping the airbrush perpendicular to the surface at all times.

This gentle misting allows the dark undercoat to remain visible in key areas, suggesting natural shadows and exaggerating the level of surface relief. Ideally, we're aiming for a smooth transition between the livery colour and the shaded areas, so it may take a little practice to master this technique with confidence. Used in isolation, it can suggest a degree of wear and tear to a surface, without the subject receiving any actual 'dirt'. The model is further enhanced by following up with more orthodox weathering processes. The cheap and cheerful Dapol wagon illustrated here is testament to how effective pre-shading can be.

Received wisdom states that we need to employ a neutral shade as a primer or undercoat. However, there are instances when an all-over coat of matt black can be advantageous. Try it on planked open wagons or vans.

The livery colour can be misted gradually in very light coats, taking care not to build up the colour too densely. Keep it out of recessed areas, thus retaining the shaded effect.

After other livery elements have been added, a very generic weathering job can be employed without the need for dark washes or precise airbrush work.

Wagon interiors can be treated in similar fashion, with ultra-light layers of various 'timber' shades applied over the black base.

The black undercoat offers a remarkably effective head start to the weathering process. By using Tamiya acrylics, this wagon was treated, from start to finish, in only a couple of hours.

Although the basic Dapol body moulding lacks the door seams on the inner sides, their location can be suggested with dark shading.

TAKING IT FURTHER

A more considered approach to pre-shading brings about a wider range of potential effects. Being able to place the shading in and around specific areas demands patience and the confident use of the airbrush. A good airbrush is vital, preferably one with a needle/nozzle combination of 0.3mm diameter or smaller. Free-flowing, correctly thinned paint is also essential. That said, the pre-shading technique can be far more forgiving of less-than-perfect airbrush control than the usual approach of applying the shading later ('post-shading').

We need to avoid creating rough areas of overspray on the periphery of where the shading colour is being applied: this is usually caused by the paint being too thick or the airbrush being too far from the model's surface. If this does occur, the dry surface may have to be rubbed down with fine abrasives and the pre-shading stage repeated.

Aim to build up the shading colour over several light layers, taking the time to build up full opacity in the darker, deeper recesses without the risk of causing runs or puddles.

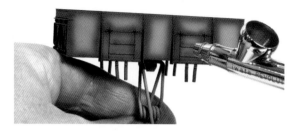

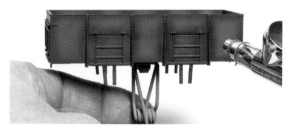

Instead of an overall black undercoat, a more targeted approach can be effective for vehicles with less surface relief. Matt black is being sprayed over a grey primer, working the paint carefully round the raised detail and door seams. Be patient and build up the paint over several coats, working up close at a low air pressure. An airbrush with a pre-set handle is helpful in this instance, lessening the risk of applying too much paint.

Again, the livery topcoat is gently misted over the surface, keeping the airbrush nozzle perpendicular to the model to maintain the dark shading in the alcoves.

Allow the paint to dry for a few moments before deciding if the shading is satisfactory. If more livery coats are applied, less shading will show through, allowing plenty of scope for fine-tuning.

The order of proceedings can be a little different to the more conventional approach, meaning that progress must pause so that gloss clear coats can be applied before decals are added.

After a sealing matt clear coat, only minimal final weathering is required to blend the decals and underframe into a cohesive image. The wagon duly appears well lived in, rather than simply filthy.

WHAT COLOUR?

Choice of pre-shading paint is partly a matter of personal taste, although it's often dictated by the subsequent livery colour and the degree to which the shading ought to be visible. Experimentation helps us to understand how different shading tones react with topcoat colours, bearing in mind that the final effect can be tailored by how much of the livery is applied. If too much colour is overlaid, the pre-shading can be obliterated altogether.

Black is the usual pre-shading choice, or at least a dark grey or 'weathered' black, especially for deep

Pre-shading is equally effective on vans and covered wagons, be they planked or panel-sided. Work the dark paint round all the raised detail and into any recesses, changing the angle of attack to ensure even coverage. For vans with complex ribbed ends, simply spray the whole panel black.

Pre-shading allows very subtle effects like this to be created more easily than by post-shading, with much less emphasis on precision.

livery colours such as red, grey, brown, blue and green. Where livery colours are light, such as white, yellow or pale grey, black shading can be excessive, so instead try a mid-grey tone, or perhaps a medium shade of brown.

A number of variables are at play when pre-shading, although there are few hard and fast rules. Indeed, this is something of an intuitive, expressive technique that needs to be trialled on a number of occasions before you're likely to be completely satisfied with the results.

ZERO PRIMING

Perhaps zero priming isn't an entirely accurate description for a technique, so I'd better explain it. Zero priming is a means that I discovered for repainting RTR stock without the need for stripping away the existing finish or applying a traditional primer coat. Instead, the model is prepared by flattening any large printed motifs or number panels, which would otherwise show through any subsequent paint layers. A thorough clean and de-grease then follows. The pre-shading coat thus forms an intermediate layer between the original finish and the new livery coats, which are, in turn, misted on with the airbrush.

There are distinct limitations to this approach, mostly concerning the nature of the original livery. Where several colours have been applied, or stripes and lining printed in the factory, there are bound to be distinct layers, or steps, on the surface, which may not be easy to flatten with abrasives.

An ideal example of when zero priming is appropriate is featured here, using a Bachmann van. Although I needed a rake of such vehicles in the early 'freight brown' livery, I was aware that examples from a later era in EWS red/gold were available for a fraction of the price. I therefore stocked up on the bargain-priced EWS vans and set about repainting them quickly and efficiently. The shift in livery shade was not too drastic, but the small EWS logos and markings were flattened with sanding pads and the models cleaned thoroughly. A mix of Tamiya XFI Flat Black and XF24 Dark Grey was employed

When repainting factory-finished models, it's not always necessary to apply a primer coat. Just be sure that the surface is spotlessly clean, and a pre-shading coat will provide an intermediate layer between old and new liveries.

This EWS-liveried van is being backdated to the original BR brown scheme, and the pre-shading will help to bring out the wealth of detail in the Bachmann model.

To ensure rapid progress, the BR livery was mixed from fast-drying Tamiya acrylics. The shade was tweaked slightly with each layer to add further tonal variety.

as the pre-shading colour, worked into all the nooks and crannies, as well as the raised horizontal ribs on the sides.

An approximation of the BR livery was also mixed from Tamiya acrylics, employing XF10 Flat Brown, XF9 Hull Red and a little X7 Red, tweaking the colour slightly to create highlights and lowlights. The need for gloss clear coats, as a prelude to waterslide decals, can make the model look rather peculiar, but a sealing matt clear coat and some final weathering from the airbrush tones everything down and blends the body with the grubby underframe.

Although the zero priming, pre-shading and post-shading techniques may seem to be time-consuming, this need not be the case. Certainly the first few attempts can be a drawn-out business, as are all first steps. However, after a little practice, progress can be remarkably swift. With the help of rapid-drying Tamiya acrylics, I can work from start to finish in a couple of hours, the only enforced break being overnight rests for the clear coats and decals to dry out.

The lack of any masking also ensures rapid progress, since the body is a single colour and the underframe can be treated separately. The roof, incidentally, was airbrushed freehand. By keeping the airbrush perpendicular to the roof, it is possible to keep the dirty grey paint mix away from the sides and ends. If any spray does stray down the body, it can be blended into the overall weathered finish during the post-shading phase.

By keeping the airbrush square-on to the surface, the roof can be painted without masking the sides and ends. Move the airbrush from side to side across the roof, encouraging the creation of slight lateral streaks, modulating the paint shade with each coat.

The combination of pre-shading and various livery tones, applied at random, gives the model a suitably washed-out appearance.

Adding deep gloss clear coats before adding decals actually softens the appearance of the pre-shading and colour modulation, as more light is reflected from the shiny surface.

After a matt clear coat, light weathering tempers the starkness of the transfers, some of which have been deliberately damaged during application to suit the lived-in look.

COLOUR MODULATION

Creating subtle tonal shifts in each livery element is another means of greatly increasing realism. Fading, from exposure to sunlight, the elements and cleaning chemicals, is a common occurrence. Also, three-dimensional objects, when viewed out in the open, tend to reflect and absorb light in different ways, according to the nature of the surfaces. A predominance of flat, smooth bodywork will reflect more light, creating highlights, whereas a planked or

These vans look so much more authentic after a considered weathering job, recalling the drabness of the early 1980s.

heavily recessed surface is prone to shadows and darker shades, as the pre-shading demonstration has illustrated.

Certain colours are especially prone to fading, with red being one of the worst culprits. BR's shade of Railfreight red, adopted in the 1980s, is a perfect example, taking on a pinkish hue after several years in service. Interestingly, the same phenomenon can be seen on red motor cars, especially those surviving from the 1990s. My trusty old Nissan Micra succumbed to the dreaded 'pink fade' late in her life, as did a neighbour's VW, as the protective clear lacquer began to peel away.

In an effort to unify a finish, it is undesirable to modulate only one livery element; rather, we must make the effort to treat each colour to highlights and low-lights, in turn. Furthermore, it's not just extreme examples of fading that are worth replicating: tinkering with light and shade can be highly beneficial in many instances. This is something that we'll consider again with coaching stock and locomotive subjects in due course.

THE END IS THE BEGINNING

This brings to a conclusion the explanation of the various techniques that I've been using on freight subjects over the years. The methodologies covered up to this point provide an ideal foundation for honing our skills and confidence before turning our attention to more complex – and expensive – subjects.

In nearly all cases, the tactics used on coaching stock and motive power subjects are simply extensions of what has gone before, tailored to the needs of specific subjects. Indeed, you should recognize many of the methods at play in the second half of this volume, so the remaining text will not repeat the fundamentals already discussed.

Modulating livery colours is a technique that can be taken further. BR's Railfreight red was notorious for fading, so after a pre-shading coat of grey-black over a white primer, RailMatch's Signal Red was tinted with a few drops of white.

After masking up the red elements, sealing the tape with Maskol, the pre-shading was reapplied.

Railmatch Railfreight grey was applied in its natural shade to begin with, allowing the pre-shading to show through. The grey was then lightened with a dash of white, and the mix sprayed strategically into the central areas of each panel to add some highlights. The underframe could then be sprayed with a mix of Weathered Black and Frame Dirt.

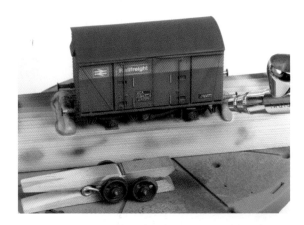

LEFT: After unmasking and adding decals, a very light misting of Frame Dirt and Roof Dirt blend everything together.

The finished results are subtle, but successful – and far superior to a one-dimensional livery application and cursory weathering job.

CHAPTER FOURTEEN

COACHING STOCK: PART ONE

Although the weathering of coaching stock involves similar materials to those already employed, it is the application methods that tend to differ. There is also a need for a more thorough preparation of the model, not least in the protection of glazing and, in the case of many modern RTR products, the delicate detail fittings that must not be damaged.

Traditionally, passenger carriages were kept cleaner than their freight-carrying brethren in an effort to attract and retain custom. Studying photographs throughout most periods of railway history will likely show the sides of carriages looking relatively well kept. The underframe, ends and roof would tell a different story, however, especially in steam days. Indeed, recreating this contrast between the deep lustre of a varnished livery and the layers of grime accumulated on the less important areas is something we need to attempt. A variety of ways and means to achieve these ends is provided over the following pages, beginning with a fairly generic approach using paints, washes and powders.

USE YOUR EYES

The best way to appreciate how the prototype tends (or tended) to weather is to take a look at contemporary images, or to observe the real thing in action. Even if the modern railway isn't for you, current rolling stock is just as susceptible to the effects of weather and intensive operating conditions as its predecessors, so there are some basic similarities in the way that dirt collects. The smooth lines of post-1950s, steel-bodied carriages may not have the same grime-collecting abilities as wood-panelled vehicles, but closer inspection will reveal trapped dirt around door and window frames or seals. High traffic areas, such as doorways, footsteps, handrails and door handles (or door-operating buttons), are likely to show signs of wear. Scuffs and burnished

metal surfaces ought to be recreated, while ventilation grilles and any raised or recessed fittings are also likely candidates for special attention.

A fine misting of brake dust and general dirt is also likely to be visible along the lower edges of the body, creating 'soft' edges to the cleaner sides. Recreating this smooth transition from grubby underframe, roof and ends to the glimmering sides can be a challenge, although weathering powders and an airbrush offer effective solutions. Consider also how real carriages are/were cleaned. The introduction of mechanical washing plants in the 1960s replaced the humble brush and buckets of soapy water hitherto employed. However, use of these state-of-the-art facilities was often reserved for prestige vehicles, with humble branch-line carriages at the back of the queue. Therefore, if you model a sleepy backwater branch of the 1950s–1970s era, when cleaning staff were few and far between, you may need to present your stock in a less than pristine finish.

Furthermore, mechanized washing installations may have kept stock cleaner, but in the early days the harsh detergents had the unfortunate effect of fading the paintwork, creating a variety of tonal shifts, and sometimes imparting a streaky appearance; this is looked into in more detail in the next chapter.

PREPARATION

Although it is not always necessary to dismantle a carriage before the weathering process, the body may need to be separated from the chassis in order to access the interior to add passengers and other detail enhancements. We may as well make the most of this and effect the weathering at the same time. Taking RTR carriages apart can be a fiddly business, and talking from experience, doing it only once is recommended, to avoid damaging any delicate locating or retaining clips and fittings.

Popping the wheels out of the bogies is helpful but not always necessary. In kit-built bogies, especially those rendered in cast or etched metal, removing the axles is seldom easy, but we can treat the wheels in situ, taking care to avoid clogging the bearings and any power collection equipment. As always, the wheel treads must be cleaned before the coach enters traffic. The coach must also be free of debris and degreased before work commences. Most alcohol-based cleaners aimed at plastic models will be safe for use on glazing materials, but I would recommend testing on a small, discreet area first, just to be sure.

Once clean and dry, masking can be applied to the sides. The quickest option is to use a strip of wide, low-tack masking tape along each side, pressed up against the roof gutter strip and carefully trimmed flush with the ends with a fresh scalpel blade. This allows us to work freely on the roof, ends and – if the coach is still in one piece – the chassis, without worrying about the sides just yet.

If the sides are to receive a heavier weathering treatment, the glazing should be removed or masked individually. To avoid any risk of damage, I nearly always opt for the latter option. The task is not as onerous as it seems, and a combination of tape and masking fluid makes the job easier. Furthermore, if employing an airbrush and working with the body separated from the chassis, the inside of the glazing should also be masked. Overspray is always likely to find its way wherever it's not wanted, so a simple precaution such as this is never wasted. Strips of tape or sponge inserted within

Unless you aim to install passengers or upgrade the interior, there may be no need to dismantle a carriage before weathering; however, it helps to remove the wheels at least. Mask up the sides with low-tack tape.

It can be beneficial to add texture to underframes with a mix of paint and dry pigment, especially for steam-era stock. Stipple the mix on to the frames and bogies, working it around the intricate detail, but keep it away from axle bearings.

Add the textured paint to the wheels before refining the effect with the airbrush. Wipe clean the pinpoint axles, wheel treads and flanges straightaway, with a swab dipped in a track-cleaning fluid.

Mount the carriage on a block of wood fixed to a turntable to allow easy access for the airbrush. Mist on a coat of generic, brownish dirt (such as Frame Dirt), ensuring it reaches into all the nooks and crannies.

Keep paint flow to a minimum to avoid runs or pooling; add a dash of dark grey (Roof Dirt) to the brown mix for tonal variation. Ensure that the paint reaches on to any footboards, and that any rough brush marks from the initial textured layer are obliterated.

Darker shades are targeted around the axleboxes, suspension points and any deeper recesses, suggesting grease deposits and shadows.

Treat the carriage ends next, starting with the brownish Frame Dirt. Again, ensure that it reaches round all the raised detail such as buffers and gangways. Then use slightly darker tones to add shading.

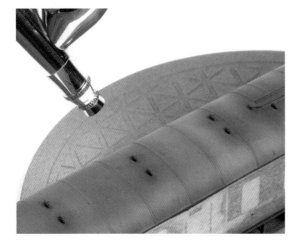

Turning to the roof, darker shades (Roof Dirt and Weathered Black) are sprayed round raised vents and fittings, aiming the airbrush from all directions. Lateral strokes then follow, picking out any raised or recessed ribbing.

the bodyshell will form an effective barrier to paints and grubby fingers!

Mounting long models securely before airbrushing may demand a little improvisation. A block of timber, fixed firmly to a turntable is an effective option. Wooden pegs help to 'jack up' the model to a comfortable and accessible height, while blobs of Blu Tack or Plasticine will hold it securely as the table is rotated – a necessity if the wheels are still installed. Also, ensure that there is enough space on the workbench for the carriage to spin around freely.

I prefer to concentrate darker tones at each end of the roof, feathering the paint inboard to create a smooth transition. The dark paint mix is then carried over on to the ends of the body, working round the gangways and steps.

Allow the paint to dry before removing the masking from the sides. A dark enamel wash is run into the door seams with a fine brush, wiping away any excess with a swab.

The spotless sides can be blended with the dirty roof, ends and chassis by carefully misting a band of Frame Dirt along the lower edges and corners. Alternatively, powders can be employed, though they may struggle to adhere to the surface of the untreated sides without a prior coat of matt varnish.

Gentle misting round the doorways softens the effect of the dark wash, but make sure that the latter is dry or the airbrush will chase the wet pigment out of the seams.

Similarly, mist a fine layer of Roof Dirt under the edge of the gutter to smooth the transition on the upper reaches of the body. A little transgression on to the glazing may or may not be desired, so use further masking if necessary. Post-it notes are useful in such instances.

This Hornby LNER suburban carriage looks good for its airbrush-applied weathering, but the roof would benefit from a textured coating.

TEXTURED ROOFS AND UNDERFRAMES

As with traditional freight stock, carriage roofs from the steam era boasted a discernible surface texture seldom captured in model form. This was particularly noticeable on wood-bodied stock, where timber planking was covered with a fabric layer and weatherproofed with an oil-based coating. Paint alone will struggle to replicate this texture, so it can be effective to add a little dry pigment and to hand-paint the roof. Apply the textured paint mix with a flat, soft-bristled brush, keeping strokes in a lateral direction as much as possible, so any brush marks will mimic gravity-induced streaking.

Choose the colour of paint and dry pigments carefully to match the carriage's livery, remembering that the pigment will alter the colour of the paint as it is mixed together. Mid-toned or darker greys have long been popular choices, but carriages with off-white roofs should be treated with a light buff or stone shade, perhaps with white pigments or even some talcum powder. The actual 'dirt' can be added later, in a more controlled manner. 'Less is more' is a good policy to follow here, as it is easy to add too much texture to the roof, creating a coarse, blobby mess. Practise on a scrap model if you're unsure about the mix ratio, and be aware that the paint will appear markedly different when dry.

With the texture coat applied and thoroughly dry, the roof can be enhanced with washes, powders and/or the airbrush, concentrating darker shades of dirt round raised ventilator pods, gutter strips, periscopes and any other details. I always apply slightly heavier deposits towards each end of the roof, where dirt is likely to be sprayed up from between vehicles or from a locomotive's exhaust.

To add texture while maintaining a semblance of the prototype livery, choose your paint and pigment combination carefully. For this LNER coach I have selected LifeColor UA816 Rail Grey and PG117 Ash pigment. Apply with a flat brush in lateral strokes only.

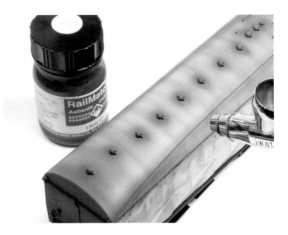

Once the textured paint is dry the effect can be refined with the airbrush, working dark stains round the raised detail and creating delicate lateral streaks.

An airbrush isn't essential: dry powders can be effective for much of the work and will adhere readily to the textured base coat.

The roof is likely to receive regular handling, so it pays to seal the powders with a sprayed coat of matt varnish or fixative solution.

Underframes also benefit from the textured paint approach, and again, steam-age vehicles are particularly well suited to this treatment. Stipple on a mix of dirty brown, dark grey and black paints, with dry pigment stirred in, and work it round the frame members, brake gear, bogie frames and even the wheel faces. Remember to keep axle bearings and wheel treads spotlessly clean.

The effects and tones can then be refined with the airbrush or dry powders. Dry-brushing or the use of pencils will pick out detail relief, while patches of grease and oil around the suspension, brake linkages and axleboxes will offer some further tonal and textural contrasts.

BLEND THE PICTURE

It is vital that once any masking on the bodysides is removed, there is not too stark a contrast between the cleaner and dirty elements. Blurring the edges with powders or careful wielding of the airbrush will soften the transition, for a far more effective result. It is all too easy to make the sides too dirty, however, so be restrained and maintain control over the paint or pigment, applying only small amounts at a time.

Consistency is also a pertinent issue to consider, as a rake of similar carriages should convey a coherent image. It's likely that the coaches have been marshalled together for some time and will boast similar weathering patterns, and with this in mind, it is worth treating a few carriages at the same time, using the same paint and pigment mixes. Since the 1990s, carriage rakes have tended to stay together for long periods, being split or mixed only in the case of scheduled or emergency maintenance.

That is not to say that all coaches should look identical. The occasional carriage looking cleaner,

perhaps with freshly overhauled bogies, can look very effective, while parcels and luggage vans may well appear rather grubby in comparison to passenger-carrying vehicles. Furthermore, the steam-era practice of splitting and re-marshalling passenger trains en route could see a motley array of vehicles being hauled.

All these methods are equally applicable to any carriage type and period. Work on panelled stock can be especially rewarding, with the extra surface relief helping to depict years of ingrained dirt that regular manual cleaning has been unable to shift, and creating some wonderful effects. The addition of authentic textures to roofs and chassis can also offer dramatic improvements, bringing out the best in an RTR or kit-built carriage.

With panelled stock I like to employ a more hands-on approach, but this means that glazing must be removed or masked. A mix of tape and Maskol is used here, the latter applied with a cocktail stick.

The paint-on, wipe-off technique is then employed, working on a square inch at a time. A mix of Roof Dirt and Burnt Umber is being worked into all the recesses.

Wipe away the excess, keeping the strokes vertical as usual wherever possible. White spirit (for enamels) or LifeColor's Remover agent (most acrylics) will help shift stubborn deposits.

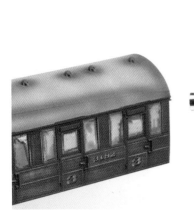

The invariably streaky appearance left by the brush and swabs is made more uniform with careful airbrush work.

When happy with the weathering up to this point, the window masking can be removed. Lift the corner of the film with a cocktail stick, then pull it away with tweezers. Press a blob of Blu Tack against the Maskol to help lift out stubborn traces.

If any residues are left on the glazing, wipe these away with a swab dampened with weak IPA, such as this formula from Medea (available in the UK from The Airbrush Company). Buff with a dry swab to finish the job.

Pick out surface relief with coloured pencils or dry-brushed paints. Footboards, grab rails and door handles are prime examples.

Grease-effect paints and washes add contrasting sheens to the underframe; these are especially effective round axleboxes and equipment requiring regular lubrication.

Although the sides and windows are fairly clean, there are vestiges of grime trapped around the panelling, typical of an intensively used suburban carriage in the 1950s.

The subtle texture added to the roof raises the level of realism, while the factory-applied teak finish is given extra life by the various layers of weathering.

Similar techniques have been employed on this Gresley carriage. The textured roof and underframe, along with the grime trapped in the panelled bodywork, provide a contrast to the bright livery.

Another example of how the deep lustre of the livery contrasts effectively with a grubby, gritty chassis and roof. The dark washes applied to the door seams are crucial in adding depth to the sides.

CHAPTER FIFTEEN

COACHING STOCK: PART TWO

Continuing the coaching stock theme, this chapter looks at more ways of recreating that wonderful, deep lustre typical of steam-age liveries, as well as mimicking the faded, washed-out appearance of more recent times. Some materials and techniques will look familiar, being tailored to suit different vehicle types. In addition a few different approaches are showcased here, such as the use of T-Cut colour restorer and tubes of oil paint, all of which can be applied successfully to any livery colour.

CREATING AN AUTHENTIC GLOSS LIVERY

Taking the deep maroon livery favoured by the LMS and perpetuated by BR as an example, our aim is to produce an authentic level of opacity, sheen and texture. Getting these factors right is just as important as matching the livery shade correctly. Possible techniques differ according to whether you're working on an existing livery (on an RTR model perhaps), or starting from scratch. If the latter, it is possible to begin planning the desired weathered finish from the very beginning. With a clear plan in place, we can omit or modify certain aspects of the painting stage in order to save time and materials.

Some of the more extreme processes outlined earlier in this book, such as physical distressing or pre-shading, are seldom employed on coaching stock, except for particularly neglected vehicles, such as those used by the engineers' department, for example. It is more likely that, with steam-era stock at least, the prototype's glossy livery needs to be replicated. To achieve this, I like to build up many light individual coats, spread over several days, until I feel sure that the colour is fully opaque across the entire bodyshell. Often it is difficult to ascertain the evenness of the paint's coverage until it has dried out completely, so it pays to be patient and to

stand prepared for the application of more layers if necessary.

Once the main livery elements have been applied, the surfaces are checked for blemishes. Several high-gloss varnish coats are then applied, building them up until a deep, mirror-like sheen is achieved. Applying top-notch gloss coats demands a little practice, but it's a skill worth acquiring, as the results can be spectacular. The high-gloss sheen helps with the application of any lining or decals, and I always seal the finish with further gloss coats. This ensures that the decals and other embellishments have a seamless, 'painted-on' aspect.

In contrast, the underframe and roof, plus the carriage ends in some instances, are given grubbier shades from the beginning, finishing with a matt sheen. For the roof, an approximation of the livery is usually enough, with darker shading added around raised or recessed detail. The chassis is painted in a mix of weathered black and earthy brown, rather than flat black, with texture added if necessary by mixing dry pigments with the paints.

Sheen is an important factor in carriage weathering, especially with varnished pre-1960s stock. We can replicate this finish by patiently building up several clear gloss coats.

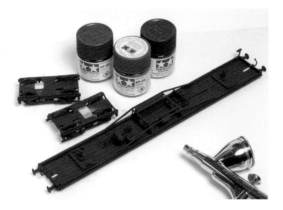

When painting a kit-built underframe, why bother with a pristine black finish before weathering when you can get a head start by painting with a mix of dark grey, black and earthy browns: this provides a perfect base for more considered weathering.

After lining, decals and glazing have been added, the body and chassis are married up and a delicate, misted layer of weathering is airbrushed on, blending the separate elements together.

It's hard to believe that this model started out as a cheap, £10 plastic kit. A mix of detailing enhancements and a superior paint job gives it an air of a high-end metal kit.

LEFT: The authentically textured roof and gritty chassis and ends contrast wonderfully with the gleaming red paintwork. Dark washes add depth to the door seams.

Although the shiny body sides will be toned down slightly, with dark washes run into door seams and round vents and raised projections, the contrast between the lustrous sides and the matt sheen of the rest of the vehicle will be eye-catching. A faint misting from the airbrush around the edges of the body will blur the lines slightly, creating a more harmonious effect.

USING T-CUT

When working with an existing factory-applied finish, a viable option is to employ T-Cut to enhance the lustre and sheen. This liquid colour restorative contains a mix of microscopic abrasive particles suspended in petroleum distillate. Various versions are available, but it is the original, neutral formula that we want, and I have found it universally compatible with the paints used by most model manufacturers. If you've painted the model yourself, T-Cut is also suitable for use on enamel paintwork, but not for acrylics.

Shake the bottle vigorously to disperse the abrasives, and decant a small amount into a glass jar.

A shimmering finish can be achieved with the help of T-Cut. Apply a small amount with cotton swabs and rub gently, buffing the surface until a high sheen is achieved. Take care not to disturb any printed embellishments.

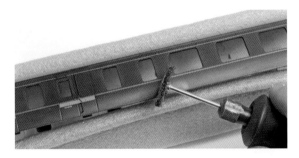

Speed up the buffing stage with a soft polishing mop mounted in a mini-drill. Set the tool to its lowest speed and apply minimal pressure.

Dip a cotton swab into the T-Cut, and then begin rubbing into the paintwork, working on a small area at a time (about one square inch). Work gently, and as soon as the paint begins to soften, move to a dry swab and buff the surface to a high sheen. You'll have to keep changing the swabs at regular intervals, so have a full tub on hand. Move gradually along each side, being sure to buff away all traces of the solvent and to overlap the working stages to avoid any streaks appearing. If T-Cut is left on the surface it will dry to a powdery substance, and this must be cleaned away with dry swabs. If the stains remain, use a small amount of fresh T-Cut to soften the deposits and repeat the process.

T-Cut is safe around clear plastic glazing. Indeed, it can help to polish out scratches and blemishes, but again, thorough buffing is essential to shift all traces of the compound before it dries out.

Although it's a labour-intensive job, the finish will be greatly enhanced. Buffing should be done in a circular motion to avoid a streaky appearance; a soft-bristled polishing mop mounted in a mini-drill, set at a slow speed, offers a shortcut. Great care is needed with the powered option, though, as excessive friction will damage the paintwork or melt the plastic surface.

Allow the T-Cut to evaporate overnight before attempting to apply any paints or washes. The burnishing work is worth the effort, making a dramatic difference to this Hornby LMS coach.

Similar results can be obtained with the use of clear gloss coats, applied after the weathering work has been carried out. Using an airbrush, mist the gloss on to the sides in strategic zones, avoiding any areas of 'dirt', such as the door seams. Ensure that the ends, roof and chassis maintain a flat, matt sheen.

We must also remember that T-Cut will happily soften and remove printed elements, such as lining, logos and numbers, unless used sparingly and gently. It is recommended that you practise on older models to gain an appreciation of how the compound can be best employed. Once the various weathering tasks have been carried out, the deep lustre of the polished livery can fool the viewer into assuming that an RTR or plastic kit-built carriage is in fact a bespoke model, built from an expensive brass kit.

Similar high-sheen effects are possible applied much later in the finishing process, using clear coats following the weathering washes, paints and pigments. With the use of an airbrush, the glossier areas can be picked out, layering the medium until the desired sheen is achieved. Working freehand, smooth transitions between sheens are possible, maintaining a flatter tone around door seams and towards the upper and lower edges of the sides, as well as towards each end. To keep the gloss away from the roof and chassis, it is possible to mask up these areas, and glazing can be covered or removed as preferred. Flat matt coats, or satin, also have their uses, and experimentation will produce some interesting and useful effects.

FADE WITH GREY

The use of mechanized washing plants, and a general decline in standards during the late 1970s and early 1980s, meant that a lot of older blue and grey-liveried stock took on a faded outlook. Parcels stock is a particularly good example, with non-passenger-carrying vehicle types in postal, newspaper and Motorail traffic being especially susceptible to the washed-out look. Passenger stock of the same period, particularly that employed on secondary or commuter services, also took on an air of faded glory.

This dreary outlook can be easily recreated. Working with pre-finished models, we can portray a faded appearance by simply overlaying dilute washes of various shades. Specific grey fading and highlight paints are available for this purpose from AK Interactive, Abteilung and Wilder. Offered in tube format, the thick oil-based paint needs thin-

ning before application by hand brush. Various thinning mediums exist, but I prefer those provided by Abteilung; different options for faster drying or extra matt effects offer greater versatility.

The oils are applied using the brush-on, wipe-off technique, keeping swab strokes vertical wherever possible. Once most of the pigment has been removed, the livery will have taken on a distinctly faded look. When combined with washes and other general weathering processes, the results can be dramatic or subtle, depending on how much of the grey wash is removed; the paints will be effective on virtually any underlying livery colour.

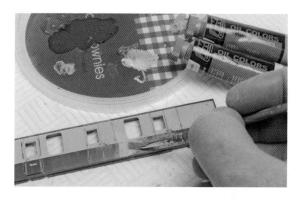

AK Interactive's highlight and fading oil paints are simple and effective tools. Either apply them in two separate stages, or mix the two together on a palette. Add a little thinner (I use Abteilung's ABT113 Fast Drying Thinners) before brushing them on to the bodysides, treating a small section at a time.

Wipe away most of the paint with a swab dipped in the thinners, working with vertical strokes. The oils remain workable for hours after application, so there's no need to rush.

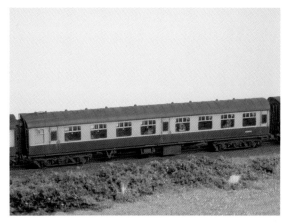

The grey shades are effective on almost any livery, and once dry impart a subtle streaked, faded appearance. The grey pigment will doubtless settle into seams and recesses, so it will have to be covered with a dark wash before general weathering work progresses.

The oil paints have helped to create a restrained, aged streaking effect on this carriage, perfect for the 1970s/1980s era.

The highlight and shading washes produce subtle tonal variations. Combined with more generic weathering, a carriage of typically careworn appearance can be created. Distressing the numbers slightly also adds character.

Visible corrosion is rare on passenger-carrying rolling stock, unless withdrawn or in Departmental use. The study of prototypes is vital to establish which parts were prone to rust, but doorways and the lower edges of the carriage ends seem to have been universal problem areas on early steel-bodied vehicles.

As an antidote to the shiny, prestige express carriages, less glamorous rolling stock is brought to life by its understated, faded bodywork and grubby underframes.

ONE COLOUR, MANY SHADES

Having considered the issue of colour modulation briefly in Chapter 13, the subject is also pertinent as far as passenger stock is concerned. When faced with an unpainted model, we can adopt a similar approach to that previously discussed. Taking the BR blue livery as an example, the demonstration sequence offered here reveals how a single livery colour can be applied over various stages, using a variety of modulated shades. Although seemingly disparate if viewed side by side, the careful blending of the shades works to create a highly realistic rendition of the real thing.

Working on a white primer base is recommended, to help the tonal shifts stand out clearly. Grey backgrounds, by comparison, tend to compromise the vibrancy of many colours, especially brighter shades. I prefer to start by laying down the darker shades first, so having decanted the regular livery colour into a mixing jar, a few drops of grey are added before thinning the mix, ready for the airbrush. The shade of grey depends mostly on the livery colour. For this BR blue example, the livery is quite a deep colour, so I opted for RailMatch Roof Dirt, blended with the same firm's BR blue enamel. If working with a lighter livery shade, such as crimson or malachite green, a subtler, mid-tone grey may be more suitable.

Start by airbrushing the darker shade around the areas where shadows would naturally fall, within recesses and below the roof gutter line, around window frames and along the lower, curved edges of the body. Patiently build up the paint to full opacity with several coats before moving to a different paint mix. This time, a lighter-than-normal shade is created, simply by adding white to the authentic livery paint. This mix is then sprayed into the areas where highlights are desired, such as the centre of any raised panels and expanses of flat bodywork, in between the shaded areas.

The two extreme shades will jar somewhat at this stage, but when the lighter version has been built up to full opacity, the regular, untainted livery shade is loaded into the airbrush. This is then employed as a blending agent, softening the transition from the dark to the light tones. Applied in very light, misted layers and targeted carefully, rather than sprayed all over, this shade is used until the surface looks right. If the darker shading appears excessive in some areas, just mist the livery colour over it to subdue it. If you feel that the highlights are too subtle or have been lost, mix up more of the lighter shade and reapply it as necessary.

This is another process that can be endlessly tailored to achieve a final result to match prototype images or your own tastes. In some cases, the finish may appear stark on its own, but subsequent weathering will tone it down. Alternatively, we can strive for a very subtle shading combination, so that

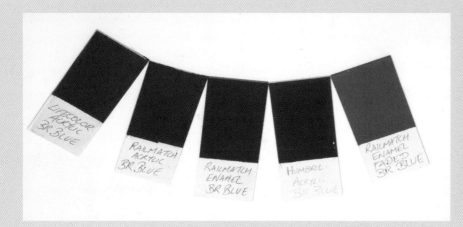

Greater tonal variation can be achieved by applying a variety of modulated livery shades, some lighter and some darker than the actual, authentic version. Here, RailMatch enamel BR Rail Blue has been altered with Roof Dirt (darker shades) and matt white (lighter).

the carriage can be finished with little in the way of grimy additions, presenting a clean but faded appearance.

This technique is easy to adapt to treating existing liveries. Indeed, the factory finish offers a mean livery shade for us to work with, adding darker and lighter tones in the same way. Other than replacing the transfers and any lining, or carefully masking them beforehand, there may be little need for extensive preparation.

Starting with the darkest shade, work it into recesses, around windows, door frames and under the roof gutter strip. Build up to full opacity steadily.

Move to the lighter shade and work it into the centre of panels and doors, trying not to obliterate the darker shading, but to create a smooth transition between light and dark.

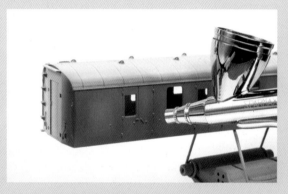

Finish with the authentic, unadulterated livery shade, gently misted over the body to act as a blending agent, toning down any areas deemed too dark or too bright. Again, try not to destroy the sense of light and shade by applying minimal paint from the airbrush, leaving you in full control of what's happening on the surface.

The effect can be as delicate or contrasting as you deem fit; this newspaper van shows how the process can add a touch of class to an otherwise anonymous vehicle, especially when combined with generic weathering treatment.

CREATING PEELING PAINT

One last potential project for coaching stock involves the use of the chipping technique. In most cases, peeling paint is only appropriate for the body-work of stored or withdrawn passenger carriages, rather than those in frontline service. However, the roofs of BR Mk1 and early Mk2 stock, as well as pre-nationalization designs, did appear tatty from time to time. For the modeller, subtlety is perhaps a prudent strategy, where previous layers of paint in contrasting shades may be hinted at, rather than presenting full-on corrosion or exposed timber effects. AK Interactive's Heavy Chipping and Worn Effects mediums are ideal for the task, as is Maskol and similar masking fluids; the latter is best applied in random blotches with natural sponge.

This rather tatty appearance looks especially effective on the roofs of shabby brake carriages, or those in parcels and newspaper traffic, and a distressed roof or two will provide an eye-catching addition to a rake of such coaches.

Existing finishes can be treated in the same way, using the factory-applied blue as a base, with darker and lighter shades misted over. The difference between the 'before' (upper) and 'after' views is stark, not least as the original factory-applied weathering looks so crude!

Carriage roofs benefit from creating the effect of peeling paint, revealing older finishes or bare materials. Start by painting the roof in the colour to be revealed, before spraying it with a few coats of Heavy Chipping solution.

The livery colour is then applied, with darker and lighter shades added for tonal variety, before the masking medium is activated with a dampened, stiff brush.

Reduce the starkness of the chipped paintwork by misting on dark, dirty shades with an airbrush.

Although not something that should be done too often, areas of chipped paint on the occasional carriage roof make for an eye-catching feature, especially on parcels or less cared-for passenger stock.

CHAPTER SIXTEEN

MULTIPLE UNITS

Now that the focus has shifted towards motive power subjects, a number of pertinent issues must be addressed. We have explored the more artistic aspects, concerning how prototype locomotives and multiple units developed particular weathering patterns and the like, but we must also consider how to treat models with complex electrical and mechanical systems.

Motors, gears and bearings all demand lubricating, and the presence of oils and grease can be a hindrance to paints, washes and dry pigments. While lubricants are fine if they're confined to the mechanical parts, oil and grease are invariably sprayed around as armatures and gear shafts rotate – or they seep on to the bodywork while the model is in storage. Careful cleaning is essential before a project begins, and the model must be re-lubricated after the weathering process is complete.

DISMANTLING THE MODEL

It helps if the model can be dismantled to allow better access to the parts that need de-greasing. However, some models can be difficult to take apart, and if in doubt, leave well alone: it is far better to err on the side of caution, rather than having to fit broken or unidentifiable bits back together! Wearing gloves while dismantling, handling and cleaning is recommended. Care is needed to avoid smearing oil over recently cleaned parts, so take a methodical approach, assigning a separate area of the workbench as a 'clean' zone, where degreased parts are left to dry out. And don't forget to put on a fresh pair of gloves when handling the cleaned components.

Naturally, we don't need to paint the gears, motors or axles, but the wheel faces, chassis and bogie frames must be clean and able to take paint. Furthermore, if the intention is to use weather-

ing powders instead of an airbrush, the model can receive a coat of matt varnish beforehand. This means that the wheels, glazing and any lighting elements must be removed or masked.

Electrical connections should be treated with the utmost care. Many models now feature sprung metal contact strips that conduct power to auxiliary features, especially lighting. These are easily damaged during dismantling and should be kept clear of any weathering media.

Dismantling certainly makes the weathering process easier, allowing wheels, bogies, underframe and body to be treated independently – though treating elements separately risks losing cohesion in the overall finish. However, as long as the same paint or pigment shades are used throughout, this is seldom an issue. Moreover, after final reassembly, any slight discrepancies can be addressed with light touches from the airbrush or paintbrush, or with a little dry powder.

CHARACTERISTICS OF MULTIPLE UNITS

Multiple units share many of the characteristics of coaching stock, so many of the weathering techniques already described may be equally valid. However, diesel multiple units (DMUs) differ primarily in terms of what is attached under the floor: greasy engines and transmissions, fuel and oil tanks, radiator grilles and coolant pipes, all offer plenty of weathering potential. Smoky exhaust pipes and stained roofs are an added challenge, as are the cab ends, with windscreens and bufferbeam detail, all of which are highly visible.

Electric multiple units (EMUs) have less in the way of dirty exhausts and spilt diesel fuel, but have their own foibles. While accruing dirt in a similar manner to coaching stock, they're often cleaned in the same way, with the sides receiving most of the attention, along with the outer cab ends. Roofs and underframes generally remain grubby, with overhead-powered EMUs being particularly difficult to wash 'up top'.

With a view to sharing as many interesting processes as possible, I have decided to concentrate on DMUs for the demonstrations in this chapter. However, most of the processes can be readily transferred to EMU subjects.

the glossy sheen may be hidden by matt paints and powders, while applied at the very end they may look incongruous. Personally, I tend to add them at an early stage, but in the knowledge that additional layers may be required after the general weathering has been applied. Besides, a layered approach is always preferable, as it allows effects to be fine-tuned. Using different shades to depict oil and grease also helps, representing old and new deposits.

TREATING UNDERFRAMES

Picking out individual underfloor fittings can make for a surprising improvement in realism, especially when followed with dark and greasy washes. A look at the real thing will reveal what colour to use for the various traction, fuel, electrical and cooling equipment. Adding a textured, rusty outlook to exposed exhaust pipes is also well worth the effort. Dry-brushing with metallic shades will pick out the radiator mesh covers, copper pipework, burnished alloy filler caps or other fittings regularly handled by ground staff.

The addition of oil and grease effect washes to engines and mechanical parts is vital, although when might be the best time to apply them is open to debate. Add them too early in the process and

Pick out the underframe equipment with appropriate colours, checking prototype images where possible.

Add depth by applying weathering washes. A mix of Dark and Brown MIG washes are being applied here, bringing out the excellent detail in this Bachmann DMU underframe.

Create authentic corroded textures with a base coat of acrylic paint and dry pigment. When dry, stipple or dry-brush a variety of light and dark 'rust' shades.

As well as engines and transmission components, greasy washes can be applied to axleboxes and suspension fittings, as described in Chapter 14. General underframe weathering follows a familiar routine, varying the 'dirt' shades to avoid a one-dimensional appearance. The paint must reach round all the intricate detail, and it may be worthwhile to apply the preliminary textured coats by hand, adding the final touches with an airbrush or powders, as preferred.

Tone down the corrosion with darker shades, using an airbrush or dry powders. Dry-brushing with metallic paint – such as AK Interactive True Metal Iron – highlights the detail on these scratch-built exhausts.

Metallic paint has also been dry-brushed on to the radiator grilles, copper piping, brass valves and other areas likely to be burnished from regular human contact.

With the groundwork done, we can apply a generic weathering coating.

A variety of different weathering tones makes for a more convincing finish, concentrating darker shades into recesses and around areas such as the axleboxes and suspension.

It is vital to keep the wheel treads and flanges, electrical contacts and bearings clean of paint and powders.

USING NEUTRAL WASHES

There are instances when subtlety is required, and none more so than when working on particularly light and vibrant liveries. Unless we want the object to look filthy, we need to be restrained with our weathering; even the faintest misting of general dirt will show up clearly on a light background, especially white.

You'd be forgiven for thinking that white would be the last shade chosen for railway vehicles, given that trains invariably operate in harsh, grubby conditions. Throw in a few smoky, oily diesel engines, and operators will be faced with a constant struggle to keep the paintwork clean. But surprisingly, white has proved popular as a livery element in recent years, predominantly on electric-powered trains subject to regular cleaning. However, back in the 1970s, BR decided to turn out refurbished DMUs in a white scheme, relieved only by narrow blue stripes and yellow ends.

To achieve an understated finish on such a light background, the use of our normal weathering palette leaves little room for manoeuvre. Instead, translucent neutral washes (as offered by MIG) feature a subtle grey tint, which deftly reduces the brightness of underlying colours. Neutral washes can be built up over several layers, until the desired effects are achieved. Raised and recessed detail,

Filters gently alter the eye's perception of an object or colour. For lighter liveries, apply a 'neutral' wash.

Add greater depth to door seams, grilles and recesses with darker washes. Apply these with a fine brush, allowing the liquid to find its own way along the recessed detail.

To neutralize gaudy colours, modify the shade with oil paints. For yellow, try a light buff shade; apply tiny blobs to the surface, straight from the tube.

With a brush dipped in compatible thinners, spread the oil paint over the surface before wiping away most of the pigment with a swab. Keep it clear of the glazing.

which may otherwise be invisible, suddenly comes to life, creating an effective, lived-in appearance without the need to resort to 'dirty' weathering shades.

Extra coats can be added to specific areas where more grime is likely to be retained. Window or door frames and gutters are typical examples. Darker washes, used neat or mixed with the neutral shade, will exaggerate door seams and deeper recesses, or help to create streaking effects from gutter strips or fuel filler points.

After masking the sides and cab ends, the roofs were weathered with the airbrush before reassembly. The buff oil paint has effectively toned down the yellow ends, while the MIG Neutral wash gives the white livery a more believable look.

Although the roofs and underframes are grubby, the bodies are kept relatively clean, yet the unit looks as if it has been in service for a while. The oily underframe detail and rusty exhaust pipes make a big difference.

For a more pronounced washed-out appearance on darker liveries, try a wash of AK Interactive's fade and highlight oils.

Wipe away the oil paints with swabs dipped in thinners, creating subtle tonal shifts and streaking effects. Note that the glazing has been masked.

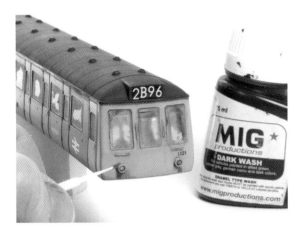

Darker washes, applied more precisely, add depth to the door seams and enhance raised or recessed detail.

Add texture to the roof with a mix of paint and dry pigment, applied with lateral strokes.

Refine the textured finish with an airbrush or dry powders, concentrating darker shades around the vents and ribs.

Ease the transition between the dirty roof and the cleaner bodywork by carefully targeting a fine spray of paint under the gutter seams.

To create exhaust staining, start with the airbrush aimed at the top of the pipe, and while the paint is being emitted – use a very fine mist spray – rotate the airbrush to feather the paint longitudinally. The further the nozzle is from the surface, the more dispersed the spray pattern will be. Build up the opacity of the stains over several coats.

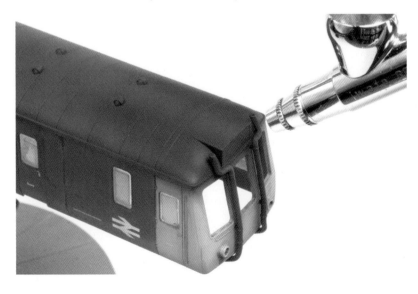

The most rudimentary of models can be greatly enhanced by a mix of grey filtering, washes and airbrushed weathering.

Modern multiple units are generally kept in much better external condition, helped by smoother bodywork and cleaner engines. Panel seams still appear on roofs and bodies, and these can be improved with dark washes.

A mix of misted dirt along the underframes and ends, plus minimal exhaust staining to the roofs, is typical of modern units.

USING NEUTRALIZING FILTERS

We can also employ colour modulation to tone down vivid liveries. Start by suggesting a degree of fading with oil paints of a similar, but lighter shade; once the oils have been manipulated with thinners, the neutral wash can be added to the dry surface. We can take this idea further by creating 'neutralizing filters', as dilute, translucent layers of colour will gently affect the perception of an existing livery element. Note that it is only the perception of that colour that we're altering, not the colour itself, as we still want our model trains to look authentic.

We've seen how effective grey washes and oil paints can be for adding fading and highlight effects, but adding a dilute wash of lighter livery shades can also be effective. Mixing in a little white or light grey will help neutralize the vividness of an underlying colour. Adding a little earthy brown can suggest a degree of grubbiness, too, without the surface looking overly dirty.

By way of visual explanation, a couple of green DMU vehicles are illustrated over the following pages, the first treated with an airbrushed filter layer of heavily thinned enamel paints. This Hornby model, although pleasingly finished, appeared rather lifeless straight from the box. If we had chosen 'dirty' paint shades or weathering washes straightaway we could have made it look tatty and soiled, but in this early livery, such railcars tended to be kept fairly clean. Instead, an air of faded grandeur was the aim, suggesting years of hard work and regular cleaning.

A mix of RailMatch Multiple Unit Green, Matt White and a drop or two of Frame Dirt was therefore chosen; it was thinned heavily, but not excessively. The pigment needs to be evenly dispersed, so the paints were stirred thoroughly before and after thinning. It is possible to use acrylic paints in this way, especially Tamiya paints, but they will struggle to adhere to the surface as well as enamels, and their fast-drying nature is not ideal. Moreover, enamels provide a safety net: if you apply too much of the filter coat or you're not happy with how the livery appears, it's easy to remove the coating up to an hour or so later and start again.

Adjust the air pressure as low as possible (10psi is ideal) while testing the paint flow. A fine mist, without any spattering, is required, and the filter layers must be built up gradually and evenly, working with the airbrush nozzle about 15cm (6in) from the surface. After each coat, examine the model in plenty of natural light to ascertain the extent of filtering before deciding whether to apply additional coats. Often, one or two light coats is enough; any more, and the livery will take on a markedly different hue, spoiling the subtlety of the effect.

Once happy with the filter, allow the paint to dry before removing any masking and continuing the weathering process. While the underframe and roof can be generously 'dirtied', you'll probably find that the bodywork doesn't need much in the way of grime, save for dark washes in the door frames and recesses.

This technique is fine for block livery colours, and we can also get away with employing it over delicate lining. However, grey roofs must be masked (along with the glazing) and the underframe removed. If yellow warning panels are present they will also need masking and treating separately, using the same principles but with a pale shade of yellow forming the filter coat.

Where this 'broad brush' approach is less tenable is when multiple livery elements are involved, necessitating several masking and filtering steps. Although a livery such as BR blue/grey is not too

Simple home-made filters can tone down overly vivid livery schemes. The livery colour is tinted with grey or white for a neutralizing effect, while a dash of earthy brown (Frame Dirt in this instance) hints at a few years' worth of ingrained dirt.

With the roof and glazing protected, light coats of the filter are sprayed over the sides and ends. Apply one light coat and appraise the effect in good light before deciding whether more layers are required.

The green livery now exhibits a discreetly washed-out appearance. The weathering process continues as normal, with washes applied to door seams, and a light misting of dirt shades to the roof and lower bodywork.

Dry powders can be effective for recreating exhaust stains. Note that it can in fact be easier to work round raised projections by hand than with an airbrush. Concentrate denser layers of pigment round the exhaust outlet, with a more diffuse covering further away.

This is another case of a 'retro' low-spec model being transformed with creative weathering processes.

tricky a prospect, the masking can be tedious. More complex schemes, involving several different colours (Network South East, for example), makes it untenable. In such cases, using grey fading and highlighting washes may be preferred.

MULTI-COLOUR OIL FILTERS

We can adapt the oil paint-based filtering and fading techniques in order to tone down vivid or multi-faceted liveries, while adding a degree of fading and grubbiness all in one step. Fill a palette with oils from AK Interactive, Wilder and/or Abteilung, including greys, earthy browns and lighter, approximate shades of the livery colours. Small blobs of the

neat paint are then applied directly to the model. Work on one side at a time and place each colour or tone strategically, with lighter greys and shades in the centre of open spaces or where highlights are likely to appear (curved edges and raised details), and darker shades in any recesses or around raised window frames.

With a flat brush dipped in appropriate thinners, the oils can be mixed with gentle downward strokes to create a streaky wash. Don't spread the mix around too much, and as soon as the mix covers the whole side, start wiping away the paint with swabs. Use dry swabs at first, then moisten them with thinners to shift most of the remaining pigment, leaving just a faint residue on the surface. As the thinners

A logical progression of the oil-filter/wash technique is to add a mix of grey highlight/ fade shades and earthy, weathering tones at the same time, building up a patchwork of tiny blobs on the surface.

dry, there should be just a hint of the faded colours and highlights, and a gently soiled outlook. When combined with minimal final weathering, the overall effect will offer greater depth and subtlety.

ADDING SHEEN

Finally, we can add yet another dimension to a vehicle's appearance simply by introducing gloss clear coats. As with coaching stock, capturing that distinctive deep lustre is an important element with pre-1970 liveries.

Following the various washes, filters and generic weathering, we can gently build up light layers of gloss varnish to create further highlights. Implying a lovely polished finish, contrasted with the matt sheen of the 'dirt', the effects can be dramatic yet cohesive. An airbrush is essential for this step, as it is important to create seamless transitions between the areas of shiny, polished paintwork and the mucky deposits around the door seams, lower bodysides and roofline.

The clear gloss coats also 'clean up' the weathering and any streaking or fading effects, softening the overall appearance and creating even more tonal variety. It takes a little practice to get the application right and to gain an appreciation of how best the clear coats can be employed, but it's definitely worth trying. Indeed, this is a technique that will occur again in the following chapters.

With a brush dipped in appropriate thinners, mix the paints on the surface in vertical strokes.

Wipe away as much of the mix as desired, leaving faint streaks in strategic areas. The oil paints remain workable for up to a few hours, so take your time. If the effects appear excessive, wipe the surface again with swabs and thinners.

After adding dark washes to recesses and seams, followed by generic airbrushed weathering, give the paintwork extra depth with a clear gloss coat. Apply in light, targeted mist coats. The gloss will contrast nicely with dirtier areas, such as the doorways, lower bodywork and the roofline.

ABOVE: **The clear gloss creates an authentic, deep polished look.**

The various oil paints have given a subtle tint to the paintwork, suggesting layers of mildly ingrained dirt, accrued in spite of regular cleaning.

CHAPTER SEVENTEEN

DIESEL AND ELECTRIC TRACTION: PART ONE

The main stars of this chapter are a Heljan 'Hymek' and a ViTrains Class 47, two enduringly popular diesel-traction types. As well as showing how two different models can be approached in terms of dismantling, and the surface preparation and techniques employed, there is also a contrast in aspiration.

For the 'Hymek', a discreet weathered finish was sought, implying a well maintained, nearly new (or recently overhauled) locomotive, but one that nonetheless was showing signs of having been hard at work on the mainline. Most of the work, to the body at least, involved the understated and precise appli-cation of washes. Overly dark washes were mostly avoided, as too stark a contrast with the clean paint-work was not desired. Instead, grimy brown shades were added to the seams, grilles and louvres.

The 'Hymek' chassis was treated almost exclusively with dry powders, but this demanded the use of a matt varnish 'primer' coat. Luckily, most Heljan models feature bogie sides that simply unclip from the main frames, allowing them to be worked on separately. Apart from the bogie frames, the model was left intact and the whole weathering job went ahead without the use of an airbrush.

ABOVE: **Dismantling some models is easy, with everything simply unclipping and no delicate electrical connections to break or tiny screws to lose. Unfortunately this is the exception rather than the rule. Once taken apart, the parts can be cleaned, degreased and weathered separately.**

ABOVE RIGHT: **Work on the 'Hymek' begins by applying Alclad2's 'Dirt & Grime' wash with a fine brush. The wash finds its own way along the various seam lines and round the edges of raised details.**

RIGHT: **The same wash, this time applied with a flat brush, helps add depth to the large bodyside grilles. Apply sparingly and build up a couple of coats if necessary, depending on how opaque you want the shading to appear.**

Delicate wash work can be extended to all other seams and detail relief. Reshake the wash at regular intervals to keep the pigment evenly dispersed.

The door seams need a careful approach, as the pigment will appear denser on a bright surface. Wipe away any excess wash with a fine-tipped swab, dampened with thinners.

Allow the washes to dry thoroughly before continuing. As dry powders are to be used next, the roof must be prepared with a matt finish. The body sides and ends are duly masked with post-it notes, and a very fine layer of matt varnish sprayed from an aerosol.

The underframe must be treated in similar fashion. The bogies will be dealt with separately, leaving just the fuel tanks to be sprayed with matt clear coat.

One of the joys of Heljan models: easily removable bogie frames. Once de-greased, they can be sprayed with matt varnish, ensuring even coverage round all the detail relief. Allow to dry.

*A mix of powders –
Darkstar (Earth and
Dark Earth) and MIG
(Grimy Black) – is brushed
liberally over the bogie
frames with a flat brush.
The matt clear coat offers
excellent adhesion.*

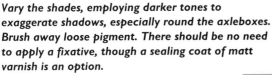

*Vary the shades, employing darker tones to
exaggerate shadows, especially round the axleboxes.
Brush away loose pigment. There should be no need
to apply a fixative, though a sealing coat of matt
varnish is an option.*

*The same palette of powders is employed to treat
the fuel tanks, again altering the shades slightly and
adding shading around the filler point and gauge.
Streaking effects are introduced for further variety.*

*After refitting the bogie frames,
a light application of powders
was given to the lower bodysides.
As these areas had not been
treated to the clear matt coat,
the pigment will not adhere so
readily. But that's fine, as the aim
is for a minimal coating only.*

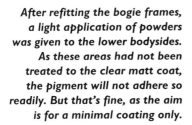

The bright red bufferbeams have been toned down with weathering washes and a light dusting with powders. The matt sheen of the washes allows more of the dry pigment to adhere. Stipple layers of oily washes on to the bufferheads to mimic thick grease.

Dry-brushing allows scuffs to be added to high traffic areas, such as footsteps and door kick-plates. Metallic paints are effective, AK Interactive's True Metal Gunmetal being employed here.

MIG's Grimy Black powders add suitably smoky deposits around the exhaust ports, with diffused streaks fore and aft. Add some light lateral strokes too, suggesting the actions of rain and gravity.

Showing that we can achieve high-grade results without an airbrush, the elegant lines of the 'Hymek' have been greatly enhanced by the combination of washes and dry pigments.

Weathering diesels isn't just about piling on the dirt: here, the subtle use of washes brings out the best of the Heljan model.

If you can get at them, cab interiors are worth weathering in concert with the model's exterior. Washes offer the quickest and most effective solution.

Add polished metal control handles with coloured pencils or dry-brushed metallic paints. Take the opportunity to paint the cab floor a dark grey, and add a figure or two. I also treat my model 'staff' to a dark wash, with much of the pigment swabbed away, leaving enough of the shading in the creases and folds of the uniform to bring the characters to life.

RIGHT: **It will look incongruous if engine-room windows reveal a clean grey interior, so use dark washes to treat the chassis block and any rendered detail. Although diesel traction was traditionally grimy on the inside, electric locomotives could also get quite grubby.**

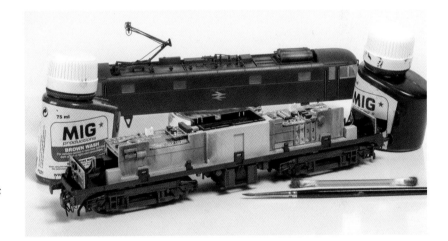

In contrast, the Class 47 was to be portrayed in typical mid-1990s condition: looking shabby, but generally in good condition. An airbrush took care of most of the weathering work – yet as great a tool as it is, it does have its limitations, and washes proved essential for adding definition to recesses and moulded detail.

A degree of physical manipulation has also been employed on the 'Duff', creating extra textures and visual dimensions.

Also visible from the outside are the radiator cooling fans. Again, treat them to a coat or two of dark washes before a gentle metallic dry-brushing to highlight the edges of the blades.

A mix of RailMatch enamel Frame Dirt and Roof Dirt is sprayed on to the wheel faces and the treads and flanges immediately cleaned. The bogies are also treated to a misted layer of the same colours.

The mix of Frame Dirt and Roof Dirt extends to the underframe too, with a gentle variation in the shades to add greater depth.

Allow the paints to dry before the wheels and bogie frames are reinstalled and detail work can commence. LifeColor's Grease Effects acrylics add a suitably oily sheen to axleboxes and other heavily lubricated moving parts, such as brake rodding pivots, fuel- and oil-filling points and drain cocks.

Dry-brushing or coloured pencils help to highlight the raised details on the bogies and frames, and scuffing and burnishing marks are added to foot steps and maintenance access panels.

An airbrush will struggle to direct paint into tight recesses, so make use of washes to bring out the hidden detail in the bodyshell.

Working from the ground up, begin with RailMatch enamel Frame Dirt, spraying the finest of mist patterns around any raised detail.

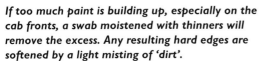

If too much paint is building up, especially on the cab fronts, a swab moistened with thinners will remove the excess. Any resulting hard edges are softened by a light misting of 'dirt'.

The grilles and roof panel seams have been treated with darker washes. The airbrush, loaded with a mix of RailMatch Roof Dirt and Weathered Black, begins to trace round the various sections and panels, adding the occasional vertical streak here and there.

WIPER TRAILS

We have yet to consider the distinctive pattern left behind on windscreens by the travel of the wiper blades. Masks can be cut from tape or film, the latter being reusable, while the real thing must be studied in order to ascertain the size and pattern of the wiper trails. Etched wiper masks are an option, produced for many 'OO'-gauge locomotive classes by PH Designs (see Appendix). These need fixing temporarily to the glazing, with Blu Tack or some other non-staining adhesive, while the weathering paint is applied. Whatever masking medium is employed, the weathering must be applied by airbrush.

Windscreens are usually cleaned on a daily basis, for obvious reasons of safety, so a fine mist of 'dirty' shades is sufficient. I usually save this task until the end of a weathering job, when the model has been reassembled. A mix of brown and grey weathering shades, commonly RailMatch enamel Frame Dirt and Roof Dirt, is then prepared and misted lightly over the masked windscreens. Enamels or Tamiya acrylics are preferred, as they will adhere readily to clear glazing material.

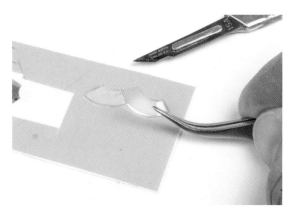

To mimic the trails left by windscreen wipers, cut shaped masks from low-tack tape or film. I use Ultra Mask film, which is easily cut, and the masks can be reused many times.

With the masks in position, spray a mix of enamel Roof Dirt and Frame Dirt. A very fine mist is all that's required.

Gently peel away the masks to reveal the clean sweeps of the blades. The actual wipers can now be installed, posed appropriately to match the clean areas.

On such a dark background, a rich shade of black is required to allow the exhaust staining to show up. In this instance, RailMatch Matt Black is chosen, concentrated around the outlet and diffused predominantly in longitudinal strokes.

After the initial weathering paints have dried, the body was scrubbed with a stiff dry brush, in vertical strokes. This creates the illusion of dirt being partially washed away by rain. The fact that the brush retained faint traces of weathering powders helped, by adding extra tonal variation.

The Class 47 received a slightly more involved approach to that employed on the 'Hymek', portraying a typical freight locomotive of the 1990s.

The enhanced radiator fans add extra spice to the weathered roof.

TAKE YOUR TIME...

None of these processes is especially difficult or complex, although proper preparation and restrained application are key. Indeed, adopting a 'light touch' with washes, powders and the airbrush allows us to retain full control over the weathering process. Being able to add a little more to the finish, if desired, is far preferable to trying to put right over-exuberant applications. Just remember, always take your time!

Small details, such as using washes on the light surrounds and the masked wiper trails, combine to raise the level of realism.

CHAPTER EIGHTEEN

DIESEL AND ELECTRIC TRACTION: PART TWO

Continuing with the modern traction theme, we can look into adding extra surface texture along with variations in sheen. In addition, the subject of filters is revisited, providing an opportunity to temper the vividness of certain livery colours, which otherwise have a tendency to appear toy-like.

GRITTY REALISM

Locomotive underframes, when studied closely, often possess a tangible texture. By using a mix of acrylic paints and dry pigments, as we've seen on many occasions so far, we can easily recreate this feature in miniature. Even the faintest amount of texture can prove beneficial in reducing the 'plasticky' appearance of bogies and underframes. For grubby machines, such as freight locomotives or pre-1970s diesels – which shared shed space with filthy steam traction – we can increase the amount of texture to good effect. Scale is also an important factor, with 'N'-gauge subjects demanding a

gentle approach, whereas we can load pigment on to 'O'-gauge models.

Varying the shades and applying them with a stippling action are important. The resulting dead matt surface provides an excellent base for dry pigments, which will serve to iron out any hard edges to the shade transitions. Creating areas of contrast can be effective. Relieve the gritty matt underframe with oily sheens, especially round fuel or oil drains and greased axleboxes.

ABOVE: *A mix of paint and dry pigment adds a suitably gritty texture to locomotive underframes. Here, a mix of LifeColor Roof Dirt, Frame Dirt and Matt Black are gaining texture from the same brand's Golan Dark Earth pigment.*

LEFT: *Stipple the textured paint carefully on to the chassis and bogie frames, working it into all visible areas.*

Maintain the stippled application, varying the shades to exaggerate depth round moulded details. The darker tones accentuate the slight undulations on this Class 66 bogie.

Once the textured base layer has dried, dry powders can refine any brush marks or stark tonal contrasts. Keep the wheels and all mechanical and electrical parts clean.

Instead of dry powders, an airbrush can take care of the blending work. Again, take the time to clean up the wheels and power connections assiduously.

Relieve the uniform matt sheen with oil- and grease-effect washes. Build up several layers to represent heavier staining, especially round fuel tanks.

Where a brush will create hard edges to the oily streaks, an airbrush will produce a more diffuse pattern, offering some visual and textural variety.

The textured mix of paint and pigment is also perfect for bufferheads, mimicking the thick grease employed on the prototype. Stipple on one or more layers, using darker shades, and when dry, blur the edges with powders or the airbrush.

Textured underframes can look extremely realistic in 'O'-gauge. The bogie frames of this Heljan Class 40 are being treated separately, with a coarser texture than that employed on smaller-scale stock.

Adding textured paint to the wheel faces will bring coherence to the chassis.

While the body has been treated to a mix of washes and airbrushed grime, clear gloss coats give the paintwork a polished look, contrasting nicely with the gritty underframe.

A closer look at the Heljan Class 40 reveals the authentic range of textures.

USING FILTERS

We looked at the potential of filters in Chapter 16, and saw how effectively they can transform the appearance of an existing livery. The technique is equally suitable for use on locomotives, particularly when a muted aspect is required. The finish of freight or passenger traction that hasn't been treated to a repaint in some time, even though cleaned regularly, will lose its sparkle over the years. A good example is the appearance of the erstwhile EWS livery that is still prevalent today, a decade after the company ceased to exist. With many of the locomotives sporting the same paintwork for nearly twenty years, the once vibrant red and gold scheme now appears markedly dull and lifeless.

While various means of filtering exist, the most straightforward option is to apply an all-over, translucent grey coat. The actual shade of grey is determined by the existing livery and the extent to which it is to be 'dulled'. Lighter colour schemes, such as white, light red, light grey, yellow or orange, will benefit from light to mid-grey filter shades. Darker, richer liveries, such as green, maroon and blue, may need a darker filter shade to achieve the required results.

Although the theory is simple, the practical side takes time to master. Judging the amount of grey filter to apply is the key to this. We obviously don't want the subject to simply turn grey: rather, the filter needs to be subtle and almost transparent. As ever, experimentation is recommended, working on old or scrap models to begin with.

We can create our own filters by diluting enamel or acrylic paints. Airbrush application is preferred as it provides an even, seamless finish, although hand-applied filters remain a viable option, behaving in a similar fashion to the neutral washes seen in Chapter 16.

Vivid livery colours can be dulled effectively with a translucent grey filter coat. Tamiya XF24 Dark Grey is the choice for this project, although the shade of grey can be tailored to suit the livery in question.

A small section of this model has been treated with the airbrushed filter coat by way of experiment, revealing how the bright red livery can be affected.

Having settled on the number of filter coats required (two in this case), the thinned grey paint is airbrushed in a fine, even mist over the whole bodyshell. Note how the glazing has been protected with tape and masking fluid.

Follow the filter layer with washes to bring out the detail, before continuing with a generic weathering job.

For lighter liveries, such as this intense yellow, a lighter shade of grey filter is required.

Still using Tamiya acrylics, I opted for XF20 Medium Grey as a filter; this was followed by a mix of washes and airbrushed weathering. To relieve the overall flatness, a light misting of gloss clear coat to the side panels and bonnets brings back some of the livery's lustre.

Dry-brushing with a Microbrush and AK Interactive True Metal paints captures the relief on the footplates and adds scuff marks to the access steps, handrails and cab doors.

The combination of a filter, washes, dry-brushing and gloss clear coats has transformed this pair of National Coal Board Sentinels.

For more contemporary subjects, the Tamiya XF24 Dark Grey filter tempers the once-brilliant red and gold EWS livery. A couple of very light mist coats covered the whole bodyshell before weathering commenced with dark washes to the various seams and recesses.

In 2016, many Class 66s in EWS colours were showing signs of peeling paint and general wear and tear, especially round the edges of the roof. Various shades of grey suggest the patches of exposed bare metal.

General airbrushed weathering completed the Class 66 project, using the tried-and-trusted trio of RailMatch enamels: Frame Dirt, Roof Dirt and Weathered Black.

The contrast between the original and filtered liveries is stark, the dulled, DB-branded '66' representing how the real things appear these days.

Some welcome textural contrast between the body and underframe is provided by the mix of paints and dry pigment added to the chassis.

OTHER SURFACE ALTERATIONS

The brush-on, wipe-off method is versatile enough to lend itself to locomotive subjects as much as to rolling stock. Indeed, this approach is welcome on models with intricate shapes and surface relief, or where an airbrush will struggle to target certain areas (electric locomotive roofs, for instance). The application and partial removal of the paint acts as a more potent version of a preliminary weathering wash, with heavier deposits left behind in recesses, grilles and around raised details. Streaking effects can be created with swabs, and some areas of the body-work need not be cleaned of the grubby paint shades at all, such as roof and bonnet tops.

If Humbrol enamels are used for the generic 'dirt' coating (No. 29 Dark Earth, 113 Rust and 62 Leather being my usual recipe), a dash of Metal Cote Gunmetal (No. 27004) can be added, which leads to an oily sheen being deposited on the surface. The effect can be enhanced by cleaning away the excess paint with swabs dipped in dirty white spirit (used for cleaning brushes). While the solid pigments settle at the bottom of the jar, the dirty spirit leaves a faint greasy residue on the model. It doesn't cause any adverse issues with subsequent finishes, and it adds to the grimy overall texture.

It is possible to use acrylics for the brush-on, wipe-off stage, but they do lack the oily sheen imparted by the white spirit and the Metal Cote Gunmetal. However, this can be addressed with the use of a gloss clear coat. With the brush-on, wipe-off method, it is important to remember to keep our swab strokes in line with gravity. The inevitable hard edges created by the swabs can be blended later with powders or the airbrush.

With a mix of Humbrol matt enamels and Metal Cote Gunmetal, the brush-on, wipe-off method offers the chance to create a more nuanced weathered finish. Work on an area of about one square inch at a time, handling the model carefully to avoid leaving fingerprints in the wet paint.

Dip swabs in white spirit to manipulate the pigment left on the surface, maintaining vertical strokes to add faint streaking effects.

If the prototype warrants it, leave heavy deposits of the dark paint mix on the roof and bonnet tops.

After an overnight rest, the body can be burnished with an old, clean toothbrush. This will activate the metallic particles in the Metalcote paint, imbuing a convincingly oily sheen. Again, keep the brush strokes vertical.

Any hard edges to the weathering can be softened with an airbrush. Home-made masking stencils, cut from card, protect the glazing.

Another shaped card mask protects the upper edge of the windscreens while the roof is finished.

A combination of techniques results in a pleasing rendition of an early 2000s-era Class 37. The shiny paintwork contrasts with the textured matt chassis, complete with oily streaks. Traces of dirt trapped round the body panels and fittings, especially on the yellow ends, also look authentic.

The unique properties of the Humbrol Metalcote paint, burnished by the toothbrush, offer similar results to those achieved by spraying gloss clear coats.

ABOVE: **The brush-on, wipe-off method, or the use of washes, is great for busy surfaces, such as electric locomotive roofs. However, the cleaning action of swabs can prove injurious to delicate detail fittings unless great care is taken. Instead, careful wielding of the airbrush can provide a less invasive, hands-free approach.**

LEFT: **Similar techniques were employed on this Bachmann Class 85, albeit in a simpler fashion. The general enamel dirt shade (RailMatch Frame Dirt and Roof Dirt) was airbrushed on to the body sides and ends, before manipulating with a swab dipped in white spirit, leaving traces around the various details. This was followed by an ultra-light misting of the same shade, to create softer transitions.**

T-CUT SHINE

The use of T-Cut, as we saw with coaching stock, can be very effective in generating a polished, lustrous appearance to a factory finish. Whether we're aiming to create a 'bulled-up' locomotive for use on the Royal Train or to depict a fresh, ex-works appearance, we can also employ T-Cut to allow the livery to shine through layers of dirt and grime. This is a technique that I usually reserve for steam traction (*see* Chapter 21), but it can also look very good on certain diesel and electric subjects. It is applied following the usual procedure, being careful not to remove any printed logos or numbers by applying excessive pressure. We need not treat the entire bodyshell – the ends and sides are enough, as areas such as recessed cab doors or bonnet tops are not worth bothering with.

Buff away the T-Cut thoroughly, paying special attention to any deposits trapped in grilles, louvres or seam lines; allow the surface to rest overnight before continuing. You may find traces of dried T-Cut, and these will need removing with a little white spirit or alcohol-based cleaner.

Certain acrylic paints and washes will find it difficult to adhere to the shiny surface, while dry powders will certainly struggle. Therefore enamel washes or paints, brushed on and the excess wiped away, will provide a helpful preliminary weathering stage, adding grubby deposits to any recesses and around raised fittings. The airbrush can then smooth out the transitions from dirty to cleaner areas and can also be used to dull down the roof and other seldom cleaned zones with matt weathering tones.

This process creates some interesting effects, especially the arresting counterpoint between the clean and dirty areas, with the contrasting matt and glossy sheens. Moreover, the look of the locomotive

Polishing a factory finish with T-Cut is a great way of adding a deeper sheen to the paintwork – perfect for early diesel types. Apply sparingly and buff thoroughly, but gently, to avoid removing numbers or logos.

Leave the surface overnight so any traces of T-Cut can evaporate, before weathering with washes and paints. Use the airbrush to follow panel seams or to skirt round the edges of detail fittings, keeping areas of the polished paintwork clear to provide a striking contrast.

will be especially suitable for the pre-1970s era, when locomotives were still being cleaned with oily rags.

KEY TO SUCCESS

Once again, a combination of materials and techniques can be the key to success, with ever-more realistic – and varied – results possible. Not surprisingly, such impressive outcomes require a greater investment in time and effort – yet there is still more we could do to add extra panache to our models.

ABOVE RIGHT: **The airbrush allows us to add shading round raised and recessed fittings, especially on the roof. Alter the shades by building up layers of Roof Dirt and Weathered Black, before adding the exhaust staining.**

RIGHT: **The attractive green livery appears dense and polished beneath the grime, ideal for diesels and electrics in the 1950s and 1960s.**

CHAPTER NINETEEN

DIESEL AND ELECTRIC TRACTION: PART THREE

In this final look at modern traction subjects we take a more physical approach in our weathering, with the aim of creating a tatty look, evidence of years of accumulated wear and tear. As well as paints and pigments, the use of abrasives and solvents adds another dimension to a weathered finish. We also consider gentler interventions, relying on colour modulation to create fading effects. Aimed at improving existing finishes or when tackling a 'blank canvas', these tips can have a transformative effect on even the most basic of models.

THE USE OF DISTRESSING

We can make serious changes to an existing finish with abrasives, suggesting eroded paintwork, damaged logos and patches of corrosion. The use of abrasives forms believable surface textures that help with streaking effects later. Abrasives can also introduce wider tonal variety to a livery, and in some cases can reveal other colours beneath. An example is shown here, where the reddish plastic of a Heljan 'Western' is exposed, suggesting traces of red oxide primer or an earlier livery.

A more extreme approach is showcased with a forlorn-looking Class 47, nearing the end of its service. I remember seeing several of these machines eking out their days on nocturnal postal services in the early 2000s. Some examples looked very shabby, with replacement parts fitted from classmates wearing different liveries – yet another worthwhile prototype feature to recreate.

Starting with medium-grade abrasives, the bodywork is treated with vertical strokes, taking care not to damage any moulded relief. All glazing and most of the delicate detail fittings are best removed and

stored safely. Work progresses until the livery elements take on a suitably 'blurry' aspect, with some areas treated more severely than others. With the Class 47 in particular I wanted the numbers and EWS lettering to lose their definition, whilst also allowing some of the red to show through the yellow band. Once the desired degree of distressing is reached, tidy the surface with a very light rub with fine-grade abrasives. There is little point in creating a perfectly smooth surface, unless that is a particular feature of the real thing.

Employing T-Cut for the same ends is an option for purposefully disturbing a factory-painted finish. Layered livery applications, such as stripes and multiple colours abutting each other, are well suited to T-Cut treatment, offering as it does a less aggressive approach than abrasives. Furthermore, the compound is effective at smoothing out a heavily abraded surface, restoring some of the lustre to the paintwork in the process. Indeed, T-Cut can produce some interesting effects, changing the sheen and tone of the colours, as well as softening any hard demarcations between individual elements.

After cleaning away all loose debris and degreasing the surface, more orthodox weathering follows. Patch painting, employing slightly different shades of the livery colour, suggests ad hoc repairs and is a worthwhile addition. The most common areas for this type of remedial work can be discovered by looking at prototype images.

The accumulation of 'dirt' can begin with the brush-on, wipe-off technique, which is especially useful in these circumstances as the pigments will be keenly retained by the abraded surfaces. Building up several layers of differing weathering shades in this manner creates something of a timeline in the

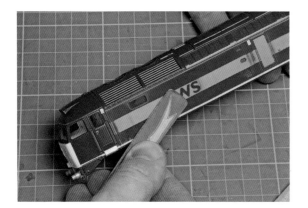

Lightly abrading an existing finish with a variety of grades adds surface texture and disturbs the paintwork to reveal underlying primer coats, or to soften the transition between elements.

After cleaning away the debris, T-Cut will smooth the surface and restore some of the lustre to the paintwork.

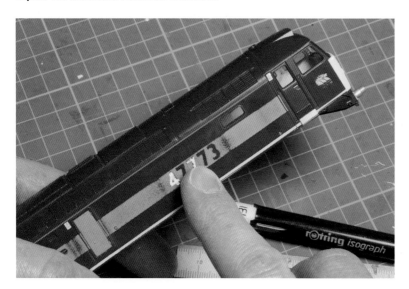

Peeling digits and logos were a common feature of EWS locomotives after a decade or so in service, presumably due to the degradation of vinyl transfers. While the abrasives and T-Cut will have softened the edges of the printed icons, we can recreate the exposed backgrounds with a fine white ink pen. When almost dry, gently dab the ink with a fingertip to disturb it and avoid too perfect a finish.

Note that one of the engine-room doors is picked out in a different livery, revealing that spares from a withdrawn classmate have been fitted. The airbrush has been employed to apply a general misted layer of enamel 'dirt'. Spirit-soaked swabs have wiped away the excess and manipulated the remainder into streaks.

locomotive's history, depicting the dirt and grime accumulated – and partially cleaned away – over the years. Refining the outlook with the airbrush, and/or hand-applied washes and dry pigments, adds even greater realism, together with streaking, oil stains and the occasional rust patch.

Having re-fitted the glazing, a set of etched wiper trail masks (PH Designs) is positioned with Blu Tack, and a very fine mist of general 'dirt' is sprayed over the front. The masks are removed once the paint has dried, and any residue from the Blu Tack wiped away with a clean blob of the same material.

With practice, the application of T-Cut can be controlled in order to partially remove certain livery elements, such as stripes, logos and numbers, without harming the paintwork beneath.

The process continues over several layers, allowing each to dry, before more precise streaking and misting effects are carried out. Grilles and recessed seams are treated to dark weathering washes with a fine brush.

The finished EWS Class 47 makes for an eye-catching addition to my fleet.

With the tip of a sharp scalpel blade we can replicate the scars left behind when locomotives lose their cast nameplates.

LEFT: The bodywork of this Class 60 looks suitably careworn, thanks to mild abrasives and T-Cut. The new temporary brandings, courtesy of transfers, provide an interesting contrast.

Pre-distressed logos and numbers are available in decal form from Precision Decals. EWS Class 60s are a prime example, many of which have soldiered on in the obsolete Wisconsin Central-style colours for years.

A more vigorous use of abrasives is being used on this Heljan 'Western', starting with coarse-grade sanding sticks and moving through to fine grades. Strokes are kept vertical to replicate the streaking resulting from the aggressive, mechanized washing plants of the 1970s. Plenty of the red-brown bare plastic is showing through, mimicking red oxide primer.

After adding new decals and nameplates, patches of fresh blue paint have been added in between layers of airbrushed 'dirt'. The variety of tones in the blue livery are created as a result of the work with abrasives.

Lighter shades of yellow have been airbrushed on to the ends in random vertical streaks. More patch repairs and the careful use of brown washes into the seams and around the raised fittings complement the misted 'dirt' from the airbrush. Wiper trail masks were cut from masking tape.

Gentle work with abrasives began the weathering process on this Class 37, revealing areas of the white plastic here and there, as well as dissembling the perfect edges of the BR logo. The abrasives have also created some variety in the blue livery, enhanced further by the 'dirt' layers.

COLOUR MODULATION

There are other ways of creating tonal variation in an existing or new livery besides filters and washes. We have seen in previous chapters how colour modulation is used, with locomotive subjects following a similar process.

Creating highlights and lowlights of the same livery colour is a task where the airbrush excels. As long as you have a steady aim and remain in full control of the paint flow, all you need is a keen eye and some knowledge of colour theory. As an example, I have illustrated a handful of different ways in which British Rail Blue can be modulated. When starting with an existing finish, I begin by mixing up a darker livery shade. This may involve adding a few drops of dark grey (typically Weathered Black) to the stock BR Blue, or a few drops of orange for a subtler tonal shift.

Why orange? Because it is the 'complementary' colour to blue, in the same way that red is to green and yellow is to violet. Johannes Itten's colour wheel is an excellent device for modellers, clearly demon-strating the inherent relationships between colours. The primary colours of red, yellow and blue, plus secondary and tertiary colours, are arranged around the circumference of the wheel, and those colours diametrically opposite one another are termed 'complementary'.

Starting with blue, if we add its complementary colour of orange, we create a darker blue. As more orange is added, the mix eventually turns into a dark orange shade. However, while this theory is good up to a point, it relies on us using 'pure' colours, which most railway liveries are not. Keeping with our BR Blue example, this is not a 'pure' blue by any means, as it contains a fair amount of green. But the Itten's colour wheel is still helpful, as we can try adding a 'split complementary colour', such as red-orange or yellow-orange. In practice, red-orange is effective for darkening BR Blue because it retains the 'blueness' of the livery in a way that adding grey does not. The other popular British locomotive colour, Brunswick Green, offers a more straight-forward subject, with plain red (such as Signal Red) sufficing as a darkening agent.

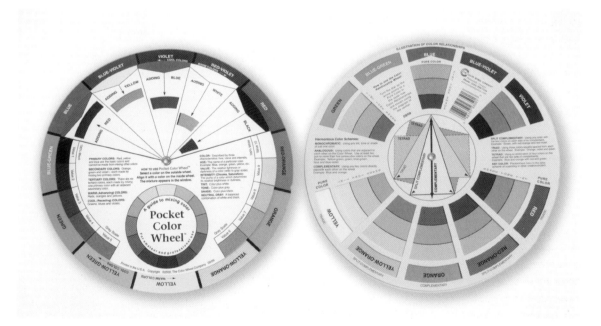

The Itten's colour wheel is a helpful aid to have in the toolbox. Showing the relationships between colours, it also reveals the shades and tones that can be created by mixing various elements.

A typical palette of RailMatch enamel shades employed when modulating BR Blue subjects: standard livery shade and Warning Panel Yellow, an ochre shade (Brake Dust), dark grey (Weathered Black), white, RailMatch's pre-faded BR Blue and Warning Yellow, plus a reddish-orange shade, this being the complementary colour of BR Blue.

Where brighter colours are concerned, such as yellow, following the Ittens theory is not always worthwhile. Instead, I prefer to darken yellow with similar colours such as ochre or pale browns. Similarly, where grey livery elements are concerned, adding darker greys (or black) is sufficient (grey is not strictly a colour, so in this case the theory is not relevant).

Although I enjoy following this theoretical route on occasions (partly from having studied all this theory at art school and being determined to make use of it), in recent years I have become either too harassed or lazy to worry about such things as tetrads and triads. As the accompanying demonstrations illustrate, there are a number of different ways to reach the same ends, so why not trial them for yourself and see which you prefer?

Happily, aiming for lighter shades of the livery is far more straightforward, with a few drops of white or pale grey appropriate for virtually any colour. Some paint manufacturers offer pre-faded shades, which saves us the trouble of mixing our own, although the choice of colours is limited. RailMatch's faded BR Blue and Warning Panel Yellow are useful if your interests lie in that era.

APPLICATION

Starting with the darker shade, the airbrush is employed to target the paint into the zones where shadows are likely to appear, around raised panels and in recesses and grilles. It's important to build up the opacity of the paint gradually, especially as we're working into some narrow confines with the airbrush, where the risk of runs and puddles is high. Keep the air pressure as low as possible (I usually work at between 10 and 15psi), with the paint emitted in a fine mist. An airbrush with a finer nozzle (0.3mm or smaller) is helpful for anything of 4mm scale and smaller. The amount of shading required is dictated by the amount of relief on the bodywork; smooth-sided prototypes, for instance, require little shading, except round doorframes, gutter strips and access steps.

Having dealt with the darkest shade, I then switch to the lightest, aiming this in similar fashion, but to the centre of raised panels, doors and the shoulders of the roof; basically wherever the sun is likely to cast highlights. After these two initial stages, there will be a big tonal shift between the light and dark

With an existing finish, the blue areas are treated first, after masking the yellow ends, removing the glazing and protecting any logos with blobs of Blu Tack. Start with the darkest shade of blue, having mixed either orange or dark grey (or a bit of both!) with the BR livery shade. The paint is misted into recesses and around raised panels, building up opacity gradually.

shades, so this must be evened out with two or three medium shades of the livery. In most instances, five shades are employed:

- Extreme highlight mix of livery + white
- Medium highlight mix of livery + white
- Authentic livery shade
- Medium lowlight mix of livery + complementary colour/dark grey
- Extreme lowlight mix of livery + complementary colour/dark grey

The medium shades are sprayed around the periphery of the highlighted and shaded areas, aiming to create a smooth transition from the darkest to the lightest areas. Don't worry about the patchwork appearance that may be developing, as this is eventually ironed out by the final layers of the authentic, unadulterated livery shade. This is misted over, in the manner of an airbrush-applied filter, and serves to blend all the elements together.

The technique is best employed on locomotives with only a few separate livery elements, prefer-ably those with body sides, roof and ends that are rendered in block colours. Larger scale models naturally offer more space to effect the transition from lighter to darker shades – when working in 7mm scale, I have sometimes expanded the five modulating shades up to seven or nine different mixes. By contrast, smaller models can provide quite a challenge. With 2mm-scale subjects, I'll usually opt

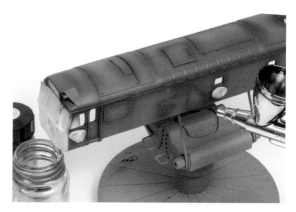

Moving to the lightest shade, mix BR blue with white (or the pre-faded shade), and aim the airbrush at the centre of each panel and along the edges of the roof – any areas where the real thing is likely to catch the sunlight.

We can add further tonal transitions if desired, especially on larger scale models where we have more room to work. Finally we can use the unadulterated livery colour as a filter to even out the finish and bring about a more authentic overall shade. Patiently applied, fine misting layers are necessary so as not to obliterate the tonal shifts. The true colour can also be concentrated in certain areas where stark transitions between highlights and shading may exist.

After allowing the blue to harden completely, the masking is reversed and a similar process carried out to other livery elements. For the yellow ends, shading is provided by mixing ochre (Brake Dust) with Warning Yellow. For highlights, white is mixed with the authentic yellow. It's amazing how much more life we can bring to a model in this way.

Following the colour modulation phase, dark washes are run into the various seams and grilles, bringing definition and depth to the bodywork, in between layers of airbrushed 'dirt'. Note how the Blu Tack covering the BR logo has left a faint aura around it, indicating that the area has been wiped clean at some point.

for three shades: the natural livery colour, supplemented by the medium highlights and lowlights. Extreme modulation seldom looks right on such diminutive subjects.

Masking up the separate sections is essential, and each colour must be treated individually, making for a potentially laborious task – but it is worth the effort. The same processes are involved whether starting with an unpainted model or an existing finish.

Alone, the modulation of the livery colours can be highly effective, giving a model an extra dimension and suggesting a well-used prototype that is otherwise clean. However, once washes are applied to seam lines, grilles and recesses, followed by general dirt and exhaust smoke, the overall effect is improved even further.

ICONS OLD AND NEW

Where a pre-finished model is being worked on, we can go through the various livery modulation processes without necessarily having to add new decals. Masking certain areas with blobs of Blu Tack will protect numbers and icons without creating a hard edge, as tape or film would. The protected paintwork may jar with the modulated livery, but

this can be softened to a degree during the 'dirty' weathering stages.

Perfect legends can look out of place on such careworn bodywork, however, so it may be worth considering distressing the existing printed details beforehand. Alternatively, they can be removed with T-Cut and new decals installed between the modulation and weathering stages. Waterslide transfers can be distressed before they're applied by rubbing the surface with the edge of a razor blade or abrasives. Some of the more enterprising decal manufacturers, such as Precision Decals, even offer pre-distressed or faded transfers, copying specific examples of logos, numbers and nameplates.

In keeping with the overall careworn effect, we can distress waterslide decals before they are applied by rubbing their surface gently with a razor blade.

Apply new decals during the weathering stage, adding a gloss clear coat to ensure proper adhesion and a seamless finish. After sealing with matt or satin varnish, the weathering can continue, thus blending the clean numbers and logos into the overall picture.

The finished Class 25 provides far more visual interest thanks to the modulated livery elements, distressed decals and final weathering layers, including some contrasting sheens on both the body and underframe.

Adding rust follows similar principles to our work on rolling stock. However, operational locomotives rarely feature too much visible corrosion, so we need to be restrained. Certain traction types did collect areas of rust in specific areas, so prototype research is important.

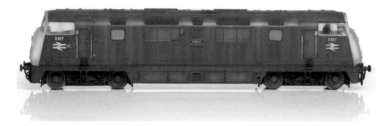

The livery of this Bachmann 'Warship' has been modulated in the same way as the Class 25, although LifeColor and Tamiya acrylics have been employed instead of RailMatch enamels. More emphasis has been placed on creating pronounced vertical streaks, a legacy of the Western Region's washing plant.

Adding lighter shades of yellow in strategic areas calls attention to the characterful, bulbous nose. The shape also dictated the pattern of the delicate streaks of dirt, with the airbrush following the profile. Tiny patches of corrosion to the valance, and the use of dark washes in the seams, comprise the finishing touches.

A BLANK CANVAS

As stated, the modulating approach can be employed when painting a model from scratch. Working on a white background is preferable: unlike grey primers, a white backing allows the highlight shades to reach a sufficient contrast against the darker shades. Again, I always start with the darker tones, following the patterns of the bodyshell. Indeed, the process is not unlike the technique of pre-shading, and in fact, pre-shading the bodyshell with black or dark grey before starting with the colour applications can also be effective, and will avoid having to mix several darker shades of the livery elements.

If the model is being painted from scratch, a white primer starts the process, followed by the darkest livery shade sprayed into recesses and around panel lines. Next, the lightest shade is applied, followed by the intermediate and authentic shades as desired.

This approach to livery application may appear more involved, but after a few attempts it need not take any longer than building up an even, pristine finish. Indeed, it saves a lot of time at the weathering stage, with only a small amount of 'dirt' required as most of the shading and highlighting work has already been done.

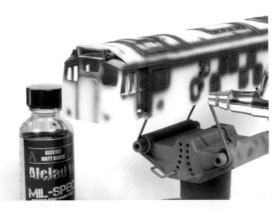

Pre-shading is also suited to locomotive subjects, especially those with plenty of surface relief. Matt black is being employed here, although only a light misting is required on the ends of the locomotive.

Work from the lightest to the darkest livery elements to simplify masking, and build up the colour gradually until the shading effect is harmonious. With the shading taken care of, try adding a few highlights by mixing a little white into the livery paint.

With the ends dry and masked, the sides and roof are treated. Again, build up the colour in light, misted coats. It's hard to tell how much shading is showing through while the paint is wet, so let it dry off for a few minutes before deciding whether or not to carry on.

With a lighter shade of the livery, highlights can be added to appropriate areas.

After applying dark washes to the various grilles and panel lines, decals were added – previously distressed – before general weathering work with the airbrush. Considering that this was a scrap bodyshell from the 1980s, much of the model's shortcomings are disguised by the quality finish.

Evidence that a layered approach reaps dividends: the pre-shading and use of lighter livery shades gives plenty of depth to the blue paintwork. The dark washes and airbrushed 'dirt' tones blend everything together.

PLENTY OF CHOICE

As the preceding three chapters have recounted, there are plenty of techniques and materials to work with in order to enhance our diesel and electric locomotive fleets. They can be combined for a multi-layer approach, or certain elements from each method can be picked out and employed in many different ways. In fact there are still further variations that we can explore, and all modellers will find the following instalments useful, whether or not steam-era subjects are your speciality.

Both pre-shading and colour modulation are techniques equally applicable to any livery and any scale, even 'N' gauge. This 2mm-scale resin bodyshell (Parkwood Models) was pre-shaded with opaque matt black, with various greys employed to create highlights.

Far more effective than applying an overall coat of black, only minimal amounts of 'dirt' have been applied, yet the locomotive has really come to life.

CHAPTER TWENTY

STEAM TRACTION: PART ONE

Steam-outline subjects share many common facets with diesel and electric locomotives, but there are a number of pertinent differences that need to be considered. Larger, more visible wheels require a different approach, and working connecting rods and valve gear must also be treated without hindering their crucial mechanical roles.

The key elements of coal, soot and ash are materials that freely stain any surfaces they come into contact with. Water also has its own impact on metal surfaces, causing corrosion, as well as leaving shiny streaks that contrast sharply with the dusty surroundings. Period is a vital factor to consider too, along with the nature of the prototype: for instance, an express passenger engine is more likely to be cleaned regularly than a freight mover. Yet even in steam's golden years, railway operators faced a daily battle to maintain locomotive fleets in pristine condition, and in the post-war years, when labour became scarce, cleaning was one of the first aspects of locomotive maintenance to be abandoned.

Even the most pampered steam locomotives, if you look closely, retain traces of dirt, especially in the hard-to-reach areas of the boiler, footplate, cab roof and chassis. The combination of high-gloss paintwork and hand-applied, oil-based cleaning materials produces a distinctive patina, quite different to that seen on modern traction. The effects of heat, most notably at the smokebox end, caused the shiny paintwork to become dull, creating an attractive contrast of sheens.

Ingrained dirt would be found round the ash pan and on the upper faces of the footplate, particularly round the smokebox door, trodden in by the feet of shed staff. Furthermore, areas where train crew were likely to climb would not receive a polished finish, lest the surface became slippery. Constant human traffic on footsteps, bunkers, handrails and around water-tank hatches inevitably caused scuffs and scrapes in the paintwork.

This initial look into steam traction concentrates on a small number of core techniques, using a mix of paints, washes and dry pigments. Keeping with diminutive models for now, the humble tank locomotive offers the perfect subject on which to hone one's skills.

BEFORE YOU START

We've already discussed the topic of handling locomotives during weathering, and many of the same issues arise with steam traction. Separating the body and chassis offers greater convenience, but also a greater risk of damage, especially with more complex models. If the locomotive has to be taken apart anyway, to install a digital decoder or other modification work, then the weathering should be carried out at the same time to save repeated dismantling and reassembly.

If dismantling appears too risky, I prefer to leave the model in one piece. Besides, the wheels and chassis frames of steam traction are usually easier to reach than diesel and electric subjects, even if dismantling is not possible. Nonetheless, to help us get the paint and powders into all the necessary areas, it's worth having a short length of powered track on hand, in order to get the wheels and motion to rotate as we work. A useful tip for 'OO' or 'HO' models is to touch the contacts of a 9-volt battery against the flanges to move the mechanism slightly, which will reveal hidden areas of the wheels, motion and frames (this is suitable for non-DCC models only) – this is also described in Chapter 3.

GLAZING

Although steam traction carries few glazed apertures, those that were present were vital for the crew to be able to maintain a clear view of the line ahead. It follows, then, that such windows would be cleaned on a regular basis between and during the locomotive's duties – although how much is an interesting point to consider. It's not easy to discern this fact from the majority of archive images, so I follow the assumption that if a locomotive is generally well turned out, then the windows are likely to be clean and shiny. If, on the other hand, the locomotive is receiving a more vigorous weathering job, then the glazing should be similarly grubby.

Glazing can be masked with tape or fluid, or a combination of both. It's a good idea to mask both the inside and outside of the glazing, especially with open cabs where paint can easily find its way to where it's not wanted. Besides, if the cab interior is visible, then we ought to be weathering that, too. A spotless footplate will look most peculiar if the exterior is not pristine.

Masking fluid is the simplest option for glazing, applied with a cocktail stick and worked into the corners, using the moulded beading around the edges to contain it. Work with the model laid flat on one side and allow the fluid to dry, then turn it over and treat the other side. Tape is easier to apply to the inside, if necessary, as it need not be cut to a perfect size to match the aperture.

Front and rear spectacle plates can sometimes be awkward to reach, and it's seldom worth worrying about getting the masking perfect. These would be the windows most prone to soiling and would have to be wiped intermittently by the footplate crew, inside and out. Even the most conscientious employee would be unlikely to clean the plate perfectly, so a blob of masking fluid in the middle of the 'glass' is often enough. When peeled away later, it will give the impression of a rag having been wiped around the centre of the pane, adding a small but evocative touch to the overall finish.

WEATHERING A 'PUG' BY HAND

Using the enduringly popular Hornby 'Pug' 0-4-0ST as an example, a multi-layered and multi-media approach was followed. Different layers of paints and dry pigments were built up to produce a range of sheens and tones, so essential for a successful weathered job. Combining to create a typically grimy finish that is well suited to a freight, shunting or industrial steam locomotive, all the work was carried out by hand (with not an airbrush in sight).

Although I have employed acrylic paints throughout the demonstration, including some of LifeColor's innovative Liquid Pigments, the techniques lend

Masking fluid is often the best option for protecting glazing.

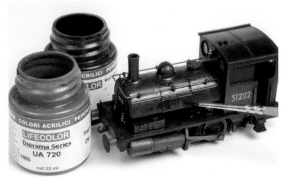

If you prefer not to use an airbrush, it's possible to employ various layers of paints and pigments to good effect. Begin with the brush-on, wipe-off process, using an enamel or acrylic mix of earthy brown and dark grey shades.

Manipulate the paint with a suitable solvent, either white spirit for enamels or LifeColor's Remover agent for most acrylics.

Contrasting wash shades help draw attention to the rivet detail.

Building up several wash layers (or LifeColor Liquid Pigments) offers wider variations in tone and texture.

Allow the paints and washes to dry before applying powders. A combination of black, ash grey and dark rust shades is perfect for steam subjects, applied lightly with a soft brush.

The LifeColor Remover is also great for manipulating dry pigments. Here the cabside numbers are being revealed, and once the surface dries out, a lighter coat of powders will tone down the bright digits, maintaining the illusion of recent cleaning activity and subsequent layers of dirt.

With a stiff brush, try stippling different shades of dry pigment on to horizontal surfaces, perhaps with a hint of rust in the mix. Grey pigment around the smokebox area suggests ash staining. Remove the loose material with a soft brush.

Relieve the matt texture with the strategic use of oil and grease washes, building up layers to vary the sheen. Work on the coupling rods, valve gear and cylinder covers.

RIGHT: A contrasting shade of dry pigments on the brake shoes adds an extra touch of realism and enhances the relief.

BELOW LEFT: With this little 'Pug' 0-4-0ST, brush marks remained visible in certain areas. Although using an airbrush would improve such things, dry powders can also be effective. A very diffuse coat of dark pigments (MIG Industrial City Dust and Grimy Black) was applied gently with a soft-haired brush.

BELOW RIGHT: Once again we see how a basic model can be greatly enhanced with careful weathering.

An advanced sample of **Model Rail's** *exclusive SR 'USA' 0-6-0, as delivered by Bachmann. I was tasked with creating an effective weathered finish that could be readily copied in the factory.*

Without dismantling the model (production models would be weathered in fully assembled form), the chassis and wheels are treated first. RailMatch enamels are employed, Frame Dirt being airbrushed initially, moving the model and airbrush around to ensure even coverage. (I should really be wearing a glove!)

themselves just as well to enamel paints and washes, although the drying times will be extended significantly. Indeed, with the solvent-free Lifecolor paints, this whole job was done in a day – perfect for modellers with limited time and patience.

BASIC AIRBRUSH WORK

The quality of factory-applied weathered finishes has improved recently, and the days of a few 'squirts' of black or brown paint in seemingly random patterns are, thankfully, over. Recently I gained a fascinating insight into how an off-the-shelf weathered steam locomotive is produced, during *Model Rail* magazine's development of the Southern Railway 'USA' 0-6-0T, in conjunction with Bachmann.

My role was to produce a weathered prototype, which the factory staff would copy during the production run. Limited to three shades of weathering paints and with a brief to keep things as straightforward as possible (to keep costs down), I also had to supply swatches and written instructions showing where each colour should be applied, and in what quantity. There was the option of adding tampo-printed elements, such as corrosion or peeling paint, similar to that applied to some of Bachmann's rolling stock (*see* Chapter 9), but with optimum sales in mind, I chose to keep things fairly subtle with the idea that modellers could add such 'extras' if they wanted to.

To mimic the likely methods used during production, the weathering was undertaken with a good

With the model placed on a raised turntable, there would be no more direct handling until the job was complete. The same Frame Dirt shade is misted gently along the lower edges of the body, rotating the subject and shifting the airbrush angle to maintain even coverage.

Changing to RailMatch Roof Dirt, the upper edges of the boiler, tanks, cab and smokebox are treated. Always keep the paint flow limited to a fine mist pattern to retain full control. Build up several light layers if necessary.

With RailMatch Weathered Black, the top of the boiler and cab are treated, concentrating a greater degree of opacity around the chimney and smokebox top. The airbrush is moved along the model, with the aim of replicating drifting smoke and soot emanating from the chimney.

quality, but not too fancy airbrush, and the model treated in its entirety. I was pleased with the prototype model's weathered finish, despite its simple nature. The mix of three different weathering shades provides enough visual interest without appearing bland. When the first production samples arrived, I found them almost identical to my initial version, which was hugely rewarding.

The weathered prototype (upper) set against one of the factory-produced versions. Bachmann have copied my instructions admirably, making for a very convincing RTR weathered finish.

A MULTI-FACETED FINISH

An airbrush alone will struggle to capture all the aspects of a real locomotive's patina, however. Recourse to weathering washes and dry pigments, dry-brushing, metallic paints and oil- or grease-effect washes makes for a more rounded, multi-faceted finish. The use of clear coats of varying sheens also offers greater potential. Indeed, achieving that characteristic oily, polished aspect is easy with a good quality clear gloss coat and an airbrush, aiming the flow carefully to create a contrast with the matt 'dirt'.

We can create a much more dynamic outlook following a basic airbrush weathering job, using enamel washes to pick out panel seams, recesses and raised rivet detail. The plain bodyshell of this **Model Rail** *Sentinel is immediately enhanced by a dark wash around the beading and window frames.*

Add further interest by manipulating the wet washes with a fine brush moistened with a suitable thinner.

ABOVE: **Scuffs and burnished handrails are depicted with dry-brushed metallic paints. Any exposed valves or pipework can also be picked out in metallic copper and brass shades. AK Interactive True Metal paints are employed here.**

A light misting of clear gloss varnish, aimed into the centre of the various panels, adds lustre to the paintwork, while preserving the dirty deposits round the edges.

A combination of sheens in the paintwork and ingrained dirt creates a very convincing picture of a hardworking steam locomotive.

As an alternative to dry-brushed metallic paints, use coloured pencils to represent busy areas, especially around cab doors and handrails.

Real coal loads offer a massive improvement over moulded plastic. However, the material benefits from a little blending work with an airbrush or dry pigments. At the very least, it will remove any shiny deposits left from the adhesive, as well as adding an authentic layer of dust to the surrounding areas.

LifeColor acrylic Grease Effects paints are excellent for building up realistic deposits on piston and coupling rods, valve gear and other moving parts. Layering a mix of the clean and dirty shades produces the most convincing results. The amount of sheen can also be tailored according to the number of coats applied.

A stippled mix of Humbrol No. 113 Matt Rust, 9 Gloss Tan and 27004 Metalcote Gunmetal adds an authentic patina to the coupling rods and valve gear. Work darker shades around the cranks and pivots.

When dry, pick out the edges of the rods with dry-brushed metallic paint. AK Interactive True Metal Steel is highly effective.

The same mix of Humbrol enamels on the coupling rods relieves the drabness of this filthy '9F'. A mix of fresh and soiled lubricants offers a range of shades and sheens. Oil-effect washes, brushed on to the cylinder covers, add even more interest.

Don't forget to be meticulous with your cleaning of wheels and electrical contacts. Re-lubricate the axles, gears, valve gear and coupling rods according to your model's instructions before giving the locomotive a thorough test run.

CHAPTER TWENTY-ONE

STEAM TRACTION: PART TWO

Making a steam locomotive appear grubby is not difficult, but there are instances when a more complex visual impression is required. Capturing that distinctive 'polished' look reminiscent of gloss paintwork cleaned with oil-soaked rags is an aspiration of many modellers. In this chapter we'll explore the idea of realistic patinas, with a number of practical approaches discussed.

We'll also consider the creation of believable streaking effects, and the issue of tinting is raised as a means of delicately altering the perception of the underlying livery colours.

WEATHERING AN URBAN PANNIER TANK

Our old friend T-Cut sees plenty of use in the accompanying demonstrations, initially as a means of enhancing a factory finish. We need only apply the T-Cut to those areas likely to enjoy regular visits

from an oily rag, unless opting for a fully bulled-up locomotive for prestige duties.

The application method has been well documented, but I must reiterate that care is needed to prevent removal of logos, numbers and lining – unless of course this is desired. Some slight softening of the edges of characters and lining can be effective, but it's easy to go too far when unfamiliar with T-Cut's foibles. Practising on scrap models is essential.

Having buffed the surface fully and allowed the solvent to evaporate, we can apply the weathering paints. With the London Transport 'Pannier' tank featured here, the prototype demanded a dark, greasy surface residue. Thick, crusty deposits of soot and filth were concentrated over the top of the tanks, boiler, smokebox, cab roof and running plate, no doubt as a result of operating within narrow tunnels. In fact, only the sides of the tanks, cab and bunker revealed the beautiful deep red livery in its full glory.

For a shiny yet grubby look, begin by polishing with T-Cut. Typically, cab, tender, bunker and tank sides, plus elements of the boiler (though not the smokebox) are all we need to treat. Buff thoroughly but gently, taking care not to disturb any logos or lettering.

With this end in mind, I opted for a mix of Humbrol enamels for the brush-on, wipe-off stage. A trio of regular matt enamels was mixed on a palette (No. 62 Leather, 113 Rust and 33 Matt Black), their slow drying time allowing for easy manipulation. The key ingredient is the addition of Humbrol's Metalcote Gunmetal (No. 27004). This unique formula produces a suitably greasy sheen, even after much of the paint has been wiped away.

The gritty texture of the real thing was also a vital element to capture. Talcum powder was mixed with the enamels and stippled on to the upper surfaces. Talc reacts well with Metalcote Gunmetal, and when the dry coating is burnished with an old toothbrush, an array of metallic textures is produced.

For the wheels and chassis, on the other hand, dry weathering powders were used for the textured coat. The underframe was stippled with the enamel mix, with a small amount wiped away from the wheels and connecting rods. As an experiment, the dry pigments were dabbed on to the chassis frames while the paint was tacky. The results proved interesting, and fitted with the overall impression I was trying to achieve.

These hand-applied layers needed toning down, to soften the transition between clean and filthy areas. An airbrush was used initially, both on the bodyshell and the chassis, adding a few misted layers to the edges of polished panels. Finally, dry powders added more tonal range.

Humbrol enamels are excellent for the brush-on, wipe-off technique. The addition of Metalcote Gunmetal will add to the locomotive's greasy patina.

Apply the enamel mix by hand. With a swab moistened in white spirit, wipe most of the paint away, leaving behind the desired amount of 'dirt'. Work your way round the entire bodyshell.

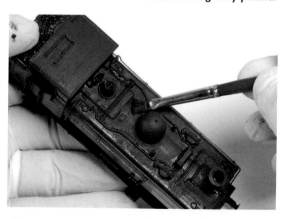

For grittier deposits, dry pigments or talcum powder can be added to the paint mix. Stipple a thick layer on to the surface, wiping away as much or as little of the paint as you like.

Working by hand produces hard demarcations between the clean and grubby areas. Blend the transitions and disguise any brush marks with a misting of generic 'dirt' from an airbrush.

Dry powders can achieve similar results to the airbrush. They can also offer a broader range of shades and textures.

The resulting contrasts between sheens and textures is one of the most successful aspects of this project. The lustre created by the T-Cut and the greasy sheen of the Metalcote Gunmetal capture the character of the prototype. Thankfully, the model's owner agreed and was very happy with the results!

It's easy to get carried away and end up with a stable of locomotives in similar states of grubbiness. But that's not always appropriate, especially if you're modelling prestige passenger operations, or even a well-tended branchline engine or station pilot.

Working the paint and pigment into the chassis and wheels creates a more believable texture. Avoid using talc round electrical or mechanical components – keep to weathering powders. Alternatively, apply paint only and wipe away the excess, before stippling dry pigment on to the tacky surface.

The vivid red has been subdued by the various weathering stages, while the contrast between shiny and dull areas is reminiscent of the prototype. Water spillage from the filling hatch was applied with a fine brush, employing clear gloss varnish.

Most of the same techniques and materials have been used on this GWR 'Pannier' tank, albeit in a more restrained manner. The textured paint mix was restricted to the chassis, but the combination of T-Cut and the greasy sheen created by Metalcote Gunmetal gives the paintwork a lovely patina.

T-Cut is also useful for partially or completely removing previous weathered finishes, in the form of enamels, acrylics or factory finishes.

Having left traces of paint around the raised rivet detail, we can refine the effect with the airbrush, creating an authentic contrast between the shiny paintwork and the matt weathering.

The T-Cut process can be speeded up with a soft-bristled mop in a mini-drill. Set the tool to the slowest speed and apply minimal pressure to the surface to avoid overheating. Take care around delicate details.

Mask the edge of the boiler barrel and paint the entire smokebox, door, steam pipes and footplate with matt black, applied by hand or airbrush. Humbrol No. 33 dries to a pleasant finish, as does Alclad2's Mil-Spec Matt Black.

With a steady hand, mist the top of the running plate without masking the boiler. The top of the firebox and cab roof can also be treated to the matt finish.

A light drifting of smoke and soot as applied with the airbrush, again using matt black, takes the shine off the very top of the boiler barrel.

The tender top, front and rear faces also received the matt black treatment, followed by dry pigments. The bunker in particular benefits from a dusty look, with a little rust shading added for good measure.

A very light coating of RailMatch enamel Frame Dirt and Roof Dirt takes care of the wheels and underframe, moving the wheels and motion to ensure even coverage.

The completed 'Black Five' represents the specially bulled-up 45110, one of the locomotives entrusted with British Rail's final steam-hauled train in August 1968. The disparate sheens and textures combine to paint a convincing overall picture.

A similarly sparse weathering job was specified for this LNER Class A4. Being a repainted Hornby model, the use of T-Cut was not possible, so the blue areas were treated to a few coats of Alclad2 Light Sheen clear coat, while the black elements were airbrushed with a mix of RailMatch Weathered Black and Roof Dirt. After spraying a little RailMatch Frame Dirt on to the chassis, the job was complete.

STREAKING

Whereas enamels are great for the brush-on, wipe-off method, their ease of manipulation actually limits their usefulness in some situations. Acrylics, in contrast, offer more resistance and we can harness this trait to our advantage whenever distinctive streaking effects are required.

Using acrylic formulas such as LifeColor, Vallejo, Humbrol or Revell, a layer of 'dirt' (mixed from earthy browns and dark greys) is brushed over the surface. Immediately, dry swabs should be employed to wipe away the paint in vertical strokes, swapping to a clean swab regularly, until the desired amount has been removed.

More effort is required to shift the paint without the aid of solvents, but this physical intervention imparts a unique, pseudo-burnished look to the paintwork. The streaking is also more prominent, with a distinct texture to the 'dirt' deposits left behind. As always, practice brings familiarity, helping us to anticipate how the paints will behave.

In contrast to enamels, acrylics can be harder to clear away when using the same brush-on, wipe-off method. However, the paints' tenacity can be used to our advantage. A mix of LifeColor acrylics is being applied here.

Working rapidly and on small sections at time, a dry brush wipes away most of the paint, leaving vertical streaks behind.

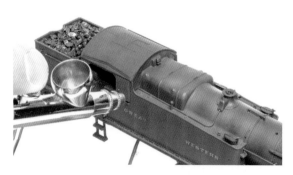

The traces of paint fool the eye into thinking that the GWR green has faded in patches, beneath the layers of ingrained dirt. A very fine misting of Tamiya acrylics (a mix of XF10 Flat Brown, XF24 Dark Grey and XF9 Hull Red) takes away the harshness of the initial stage.

A darker mix (Tamiya XF1 Flat Black, XF24 Dark Grey and XF10 Flat Brown) is concentrated round the smokebox, footplate, cab and bunker. Moving nearer to a pure matt black, smoke and soot staining is misted over the top of the boiler and cab roof.

With a careful aim and vertical strokes, clear gloss is sprayed into the centre of each riveted tank panel. A few light layers are built up until the desired sheen is created. Keep the gloss away from the rivets and tank edges to preserve the matt 'dirt'.

A few glossy patches in the centre of each boiler section and on the edges of the firebox finish the job.

If the streaks are too faint, allow the surface to dry before repeating the process with a slightly modified shade. If the effects are too stark, clean up with white spirit or Lifecolor Remover and start again.

A GLOSS FINISH

The alternative to T-Cut is a clear gloss coat, applied towards the end of the weathering process. The results can be similar, and the lack of buffing saves an hour or two of labour. Where the T-Cut method has the advantage is in the ease of application, where accuracy is not important. With clear coats, however, precision is vital. Simply covering the whole model in gloss varnish won't have the desired effect, so airbrushing is the only viable means of application. By targeting only those areas likely to have been cleaned assiduously – cab, tender and tank sides, boiler barrel, splashers and smoke deflectors – the contrast with the duller, untreated surfaces can be highly effective.

It's essential to aim the gloss coat carefully so as to preserve the matt sheen of the grubbier areas. By controlling the paint flow, it is possible to build up very light layers, adding more coats until the desired level of shine is achieved. If you don't want too much glossy texture, try a satin formula instead. One of

With acrylics used throughout, it didn't take long for this Hornby model to take on a much more convincing air.

The partially removed LifeColor paints and the later gloss coats create a subtle yet eye-catching patina.

Without the hand-applied layers of paint, this 2-8-0T lacks a little in terms of texture, but the addition of clear gloss coats ensures an acceptable level of authenticity. Tamiya acrylics have been employed throughout, except for the cylinders and connecting rods. The latter were treated with LifeColor Grease Effects paints.

This Hornby Fowler 2-6-4T was treated with the same materials and techniques as the green GWR 2-8-2T. Clear gloss coats have given the flush tank and cab sides a real lift, contrasting with the dusty expanse of the boiler, smokebox and chassis.

the reasons why I'm a fan of the Alclad2 range of clear coats is the choice of sheens available; Light Sheen is a useful alternative to the gloss coating.

Another interesting use for clear gloss coats is their ability to 'clean up' a weathered surface. Previous layers of paint or dry pigments can be rendered less visible, therefore offering greater subtlety. Try it for yourself to see how it works. As an illustration, the tank sides of the Fowler 2-6-4T pictured here were almost as dusty looking as the boiler barrel prior to a few coats of clear gloss.

If precise airbrush application is not possible, we can apply an overall gloss coat (by hand, aerosol or airbrush) at the outset. The choice of clear coat formula will be important, as subsequent work with weathering paints, washes, solvents and physical contact from swabs or stiff brushes, may soften or remove the varnish. For example, a resilient acrylic clear coat is recommended if you intend to employ enamel paints and washes as it will be impermeable to solvents, provided that it has cured fully beforehand.

TINTING

Tinting is a useful process to keep in reserve, especially when tasked with the rendition of a virtually pristine locomotive. The process involves adding a drop or two of black paint to a clear varnish, which is then applied over the entire model. This effectively tempers bright colours, and the degree of tinting is governed by how much black is added and how many coats are applied. We can even dull certain areas of the model more than others, if desired, with extra layers of the tinted varnish.

While it is especially effective on vivid liveries, such as apple green, yellow, blue and red, it's also great for black locomotives where it takes the edge off bright numerals, logos and lining. It need only be a minor tint in most cases, just enough to soften the contrast between bright and dark colours. The process is especially effective when the clear coat sheen is also tailored to different areas: glossy for the cab sides and boiler, matt for the smokebox and running plate.

Be certain that the paint and clear coat formulas are compatible. RailMatch enamel paints and varnishes work very well together, as do those from Phoenix. I've never tried acrylics in this situation so can't recommend any combinations with absolute confidence, other than Tamiya paints and clear coat.

Don't forget that weathering isn't just about dirtying the model — it also involves the evocation of atmosphere. Creating a fleet of steam locomotives that blend effortlessly into their surroundings is our aim. Including plenty of variety, in terms of sheen and texture, is as important as the amount of 'dirt' that each engine carries.

The techniques outlined here allow for almost endless variations to suit a great many locomotive types, liveries and periods. They also translate equally well to any scale.

Try adding a drop or two of black paint to a clear coat before application. This will temper vivid livery colours or bright numbers and logos. This 'before' (upper) and 'after' view reveals how subtle the transformation can be.

CHAPTER TWENTY-TWO

STEAM TRACTION: PART THREE

One might think that a plain black steam locomotive wouldn't hold much potential for the avid weathering enthusiast: surely there's much more fun to be had with coloured liveries, buffed paintwork and distressed lining. Yet I often find myself spending more time and effort on subjects of a humble nature. The explanation for this lies in the fact that black locomotives were more likely to be employed on freight work, and as a consequence, would be further down the roster for daily cleaning, especially in the post-war era. Naturally this means a greater need for dirt, grime and dust to be layered on to the model, perhaps with patches of corrosion and limescale staining.

A less obvious rationale for my extra efforts is the urge to do something different. Black steam traction did not always appear filthy and unkempt, so a more nuanced approach may sometimes be necessary. The onus should not always be on dirt. The use of textures, sheens, highlights and shading – all processes that we've seen in action already – is worth considering.

ESTABLISHING LIGHT AND SHADE

It took some time for me to feel happy treating a steam locomotive to airbrushed highlights and shading, although in retrospect, I wondered why I'd put it off for so long. Indeed, the process lends itself perfectly to the profile and contours of steam traction. Boiler barrels, domes, fireboxes and smokeboxes all provide plenty of surfaces around which we can create shadows and highlights. Splashers, running plates, cabs, bunkers and tenders, with plenty of rivet detail and individual panels, also add to the potential. My first efforts were confined to cheap plastic kits, particularly those ex-Airfix/Kitmaster steam subjects currently

in the Dapol range: quite a few of the '9F' kits were roughly stuck together and used as guinea pigs before I felt confident enough to work on more expensive RTR models.

The procedure follows the same path as previously described, with the darkest shades being concentrated into recesses and around raised fittings. Gradually lighter shades drift towards the centre of panels and the upper edges of bunkers, firebox and cab. The results bring greater emphasis to the model's shape and relief. The choice of colours is down to personal judgement and study of the real thing (or similar prototypes). In general, a variety of mid-to-dark greys, with a dash of earthy brown and matt black, will suffice. The black is seldom used on its own, but is employed to create the darkest shading tones. If desired, more brown (such as a generic Frame Dirt weathering shade) can be added to the mix, although I aim to keep the application of the 'muck' until later, when it can be controlled more effectively.

The type of paint is not important, although I've enjoyed using RailMatch enamels or Tamiya acrylics in particular. Alclad2's Mil-Spec ready-to-spray enamels have also proved excellent, with a variety of military camouflage and uniform colours being

We can inject a great deal of life into a plain black livery without simply resorting to the application of 'dirty' brown colours. A cheap or scrap model, primed in grey, offers a perfect canvas on which to practise shading and highlighting with an airbrush.

When starting with an existing black finish, begin with a mix of matt black and dark grey (I'm using Alclad2 Mil-Spec No. 102 Matt Black and 215 Black-Grey) and spray a fine mist into the recesses and against the edges of raised fittings – wherever shadows are likely to fall on the real thing. Keep paint flow to a minimum, and set the air pressure to around 15psi.

Move to a lighter shade of grey, depending on how faded you want the livery to appear. RailMatch Roof Dirt is an option, but I'm using Alclad2 Mil-Spec No. 250 Panzer Schwartzgrau in this instance. Work the paint into the centre of the boiler sections, cylinder covers, cab side panels and other zones where highlights ought to appear.

The three shades of Alclad2 Mil-Spec enamel combine to create a range of useful tones. A small amount of No. 021 RAF Dark Earth was also added to the mix, to give just a hint of 'dirt'.

Now move to a shade approximately halfway between the two previously applied colours, and use the airbrush to smooth out the transitions between highlights and shading.

Although there's still more work to do, the transformation from the factory finish (upper) is dramatic.

After gentle, more orthodox weathering, the finished model looks anything but one-dimensional.

The tender can be treated in similar fashion. This riveted Stanier example offers many shading and highlighting opportunities. The darker tones can follow the patterns of raised detail.

A similar approach can be adopted when painting a model from scratch. After a grey primer, the process follows the same procedure, with the darkest shade applied first. Tamiya acrylics are used here.

When treating a locomotive in separate sections, be sure to check for consistency in the various shades employed. Gentle, darker vertical streaks relieve the flatness of this slab-sided tender.

Four shades of Tamiya acrylics – XF10 Flat Brown, XF52 Flat Earth, XF24 Dark Grey and a hint of XF1 Flat Black – combine to enhance this Bachmann 'ROD' 2-8-0 in typically weatherbeaten War Department condition.

For a more unkempt locomotive, we can abandon caution and apply plentiful airbrushed layers of the usual shades: RailMatch Frame Dirt, Roof Dirt and Weathered Black. Adding vertical streaks in different tones gives an extra dimension to the weathering.

Move the airbrush to follow the profile of the locomotive, working the paint evenly around all protrusions and recesses, being careful to emit only a fine misted spray pattern at all times.

perfect for the job. The paint must be applied gradually, in a fine, controlled mist. We don't have to begin with an existing black livery, by the way, as the process is just as easy to follow when starting with a grey primer coat.

A little experimentation is needed to appreciate the possibilities of this process, which is why I began with cheap plastic kits as a learning tool. Hopefully the models showcased here illustrate the potential and effectiveness of the technique.

RENDERING RUST

A characteristic feature of old steam locomotives was corroded steel showing through peeling paint, especially around the smokebox. Furthermore, as valuable cast name and number plates were removed from engines still in service, rusty patches were revealed.

We can apply corrosion stains on to the paintwork easily enough, with paints, pigments or even coloured pencils or pastels. However, rendering the rust under blistering paint is far more authentic and is a surprisingly attainable goal. After stippling on a mix of rusty red-brown paints to the sides and front of the smokebox, perhaps with a little dry pigment mixed in for texture, masking fluid is sponged on in random blotches.

After over-painting the smokebox, by hand or airbrush, with a flat mix of matt black, dark grey and a drop of earth brown (RailMatch Matt Black, Weathered Black and Frame Dirt for example), the masking fluid can be removed. With judicious use of a stiff brush we can peel the fluid away, revealing the 'rust' beneath blistered and flaking paint.

Where name and number plates were removed, patches of rust would be revealed. We can recreate these with artists' coloured pencils. Use a variety of shades, and blend them together on the surface with a fingertip or a dry cotton swab.

Use a fine scriber point or an embroidery needle to punch bolt holes from the missing plates.

Dry pigments are the best for depicting deposits of soot, ash and coal dust.

This withdrawn ex-LNER 'B1' has been reactivated for departmental service, albeit in very shabby external condition.

Scorched, peeling paint from smokeboxes became a common sight in the 1960s. Stipple a range of rust shades on to the model smokebox, dabbing with a dry swab to add some authentic texture.

When dry, apply masking fluid in random blobs, preferably with a scrap of sponge.

When the masking fluid has cured, the whole smokebox can be painted by hand or airbrush.

Remove the mask with a stiff-bristled brush, encouraging the edges of the paint to peel.

Temper the vivid rust patches with a misting of general 'dirt' (Roof Dirt/Weathered Black) from the airbrush, or apply a light covering of dry pigments.

This end-of-steam '8F' has received several layers of paints and dry pigments, as well as glossy oil- and grease-effect washes, creating a wide range of tones, sheens and textures. The peeling paint and rusty deposits add yet another dimension.

CREATING LIMESCALE STREAKS

Adding limescale streaks, emanating from boiler wash-out plugs and feed valves, is possible in a number of ways. Paints and pigments are suitable, applied by hand or sprayed carefully through an airbrush. Layering the stains, using slightly different shades of paint or pigment, produces effective results, suggesting a longer period of accumulation, and prototype study is important to discern where the streaks would most likely appear and to what extent. Simply applying white paint, as some ready-weathered models have done in the past, never looks convincing. Instead, creamy, stone-coloured shades are more appropriate.

Employing an airbrush for this task demands perfect control over the paint flow and accurate aim of the nozzle. The paint must be mixed and thinned to a high standard, and the airbrush in optimum working order. Any minor blockages, or uneven airflow, will ruin the effect. A tool with a fine needle/nozzle combination is essential, with 0.3mm or smaller being preferred.

Limescale streaking, emanating mostly from boiler wash-out plugs, is a worthwhile feature to reproduce. The easiest method is to employ off-white paint and a fine brush.

Hand-applied staining can appear a little stark unless toned down with subsequent weathering from the airbrush or dry powders.

It's a good idea to practise on an old model, or better still, on a sheet of card. Draw a row of dots and work to perfect your aim, so that the paint lands exactly where you want it to. The flow of paint and gentle downward movement of the airbrush should also be rehearsed over and over again, until you can describe subtle, straight streaks emanating from each dot. Ideally, the streaks need to taper off at their extremity, which requires deft toggling of the airbrush trigger. With a double-action airbrush, the operating procedure is as follows:

- Aim the nozzle at the washout plug (or wherever the streak is to begin)
- Depress the trigger so that only air is being emitted
- Slowly pull the trigger backwards
- As soon as the paint appears on the surface, move the airbrush downwards in a gentle movement
- At the desired point, push the trigger forwards to cut off the paint while the airbrush is still moving
- Keep the trigger depressed for a second or so before releasing it

Keeping the air 'on' after the paint has been shut off, prevents any fluid remaining on the end of the needle. If this occurs, then as soon as the trigger is pressed again, the paint on the needle is blown on to the model in a rough spatter.

Repeat the process to build up the desired degree of opacity, perhaps tweaking the paint shade slightly for extra realism. Working with your elbows resting on the workbench helps to keep the airbrush steady, and using an airbrush with a paint flow limiter (pre-set handle) will reduce the risk of applying too much paint at the wrong moment.

Don't worry about handrails, reversing rods or pipework that may be in the way of the streaks, even if they ought to remain free of the staining. They can be touched in later with the livery or weathering shades.

It helps to mist over a very fine layer of general 'muck' to temper the streaks. Therefore, I instigate the limescale stage after most of the general weathering has been applied, but before the final touches are added, so that everything can be blended together.

I hope this chapter has shown that plain old black locomotives can be anything but boring. They offer many great creative opportunities, and some of the aspects touched upon here will be developed further in the next section.

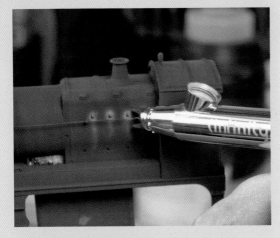

A good quality airbrush can take care of fine streaking effects, although it takes practice to get the paint exactly where you want it. Work with the nozzle close to the surface; a crown-shaped rim helps by minimizing blow-back.

Handrails and other fittings inevitably get in the way, but with a scrap of paper to protect the streaks, the parts can be touched up.

Create a more harmonious effect by toning down the streaks with a fine misted layer of weathering.

A crisis becomes an opportunity! Having accidentally scratched the weathered finish, I decided to add a little 'graffiti' with the end of a cocktail stick. Instead of the obvious 'Clean Me!' slogan, I opted for something more sarcastic.

Having been inspired by contemporary colour images, I gave this Bachmann 'WD' a textured, greasy underframe and an array of airbrushed shades, including traces of limescale staining. RailMatch and Humbrol enamels were used throughout, with dry pigments giving key areas a suitably dusty sheen.

CHAPTER TWENTY-THREE

STEAM TRACTION: PART FOUR

This final chapter, of the four devoted to steam traction and of the book itself, offers a selection of techniques, some of which could be considered rather unorthodox. The theories of pre-shading, colour modulation and chipping effects have been covered elsewhere, but the following projects illustrate how these unorthodox methods can be translated effectively to steam subjects.

Some processes may only be appropriate for niche applications, such as a particularly decrepit industrial or withdrawn mainline locomotive.

Similarly, the modulation of steam-era liveries to create highlight and lowlight effects may infuriate some purists. However, these are valid undertakings, and are presented in order to give readers a clear idea of what is possible, especially when more creative approaches are adopted.

It's easy – and tempting – to follow the same old ways and means, remaining firmly in your comfort zone. Indeed, there's nothing wrong with constantly practising until you feel confident and familiar with certain materials and methods. Yet trying new

When repainting a locomotive, try employing the pre-shading technique to add some extra depth to a finish. Models with plenty of relief are especially rewarding to work on, particularly tenders with rows of rivet detail.

Steam locomotives offer plenty of contours into which the pre-shading coats can be targeted.

Begin layering the livery coats patiently, so as to preserve the depth of shading.

Target the spray pattern carefully to ensure a smooth transition between lighter and darker tones, adding further layers of colour over any areas where the shading appears too stark. Remember to let the paint go off slightly in order to better appreciate how the shading appears.

With pre-shading, there is less need to modify the livery colour to a darker tone, but we can create lighter versions with the addition of white paint.

Remember that the airbrush should only be emitting a fine, controllable mist at all times, and be careful not to build up the colour on the model too quickly.

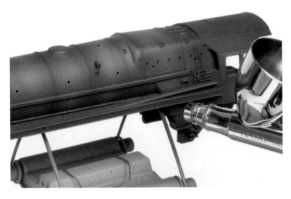

Pick out the central areas of each section with the lighter shade, together with the top of the firebox and other areas where highlights are likely to appear. The fine mist will allow for a smooth shift between shades.

The lighter shade, aimed into the middle of each riveted panel, soon brings the surface to life.

Pre-shading should be extended to all elements of a livery, including the bufferbeams, for a more coherent finish.

A stress-free option is to practise on a spare bodyshell or cheap plastic kit. If you're not happy, simply start again by spraying on another coat of acrylic primer.

things can be fun and exciting, helping to rejuvenate enthusiasm. Furthermore, you might find a fresh way of achieving your goals that is quicker or easier than before.

'Thinking outside the box' has become an over-used cliché, but retaining an open mind and a creative curiosity has certainly helped me to maintain my modelling enthusiasm, despite my hobby having become my profession. As a result, even after a couple of decades, I still can't wait to start work every morning, especially when a new project is about to begin.

I sincerely hope that this book fills you with a similar fervour for trying out new materials and techniques, inspiring you to head back to the workbench and start on your next modelling endeavour. Enjoy it!

The colour of the primer and the extent of the pre-shading dictates how vivid the final livery will appear. White primer is used for this GWR 2-8-0, with matt black for the pre-shading coats.

The green appears brighter on the white background, but we need to ensure that the shift towards the shaded areas is smooth. Keep building up the livery until you are happy with the transition, taking care not to eradicate the shadow effect.

With a slightly lighter mix of GWR green (add white), highlights are added, reinstating the vivid outlook away from the shaded areas. Again, keep the transition between tones as seamless as possible.

The tender boasts plenty of rivet detail, as well as raised beading and curved contours, offering a great deal of potential for creating shaded effects.

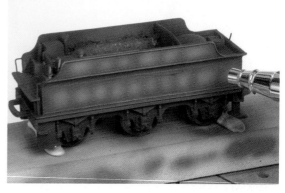

Once the lighter shade is added too, we are treated with a more three-dimensional appearance.

After masking and painting the other livery elements, a number of clear gloss coats are built up ready for the waterslide decals. The clear coats actually diminish somewhat the extent of the shading and highlights, creating a more harmonious form.

The oily patina of this much rebuilt Hornby model perfectly evokes the appearance of a well kept freight engine of the inter-war period.

After partial dismantling, the rear bulkhead was distressed with pliers, followed by stippling with liquid poly cement. The resultant texture and damaged appearance capture the effects of rough loading with coal over the years. Leave overnight to harden completely.

Generic airbrush weathering work followed, using Tamiya acrylics. Much of the glossy sheen was retained in certain areas, giving a distinctive polished look and contrasting with the matt smokebox, running plate and underframe.

Industrial locomotives could take on a melancholic air when their days were nearly up. This Ixion 'O'-gauge Hudswell Clarke 0-6-0ST is ready for some robust weathering!

Three different shades of Modelmates Rust Effects dye were brushed on in thick coats, in several layers, to build up a realistic texture and tones.

The Modelmates dyes remain re-workable unless sealed, so a few coats of clear matt were sprayed over the treated areas.

AK Interactive's Heavy Chipping medium was airbrushed over the areas of corrosion, in three separate coats.

The cab, bunker and saddle tanks were sprayed with a darker shade of green. It is essential that water-based acrylic paint is employed, so I chose a pot of LifeColor.

The smokebox, running plate and cab roof also received a coating of LifeColor acrylic, this time using Weathered Black.

When the paints had dried, a damp, stiff brush softened the Heavy Chipping medium and revealed the corrosion and original livery shades.

The surface was allowed to dry out before sealing with clear satin coats. A mix of acrylics and dry pigments added some rough texture to the wheels and underframe.

Before reassembly, the cab interior was treated with paints, washes and dry powders. The crew figures were given a dark wash, so they too would blend in with the dirt-laden surroundings.

After layers of washes were brushed over the bodywork and chassis, all the individual weathering stages were unified by a light misting of various shades of Tamiya acrylics.

In terms of peeling paint, corrosion, gritty texture and contrasting sheens there's a great deal going on, yet nothing stands out as being incongruous.

As well as the realistic texture and tones created by the Modelmates dyes, the traces of previous livery colours add even more to this locomotive's unique story.

Physical distressing of the bunker and rear cab bulkhead help make sense of the heavily corroded steelwork. Such a rusty finish to an otherwise pristine bodyshell would look wrong, especially in a large scale such as 'O' gauge.

LIST OF SUPPLIERS

The Airbrush Company
79 Marlborough Road, Lancing Business Park,
West Sussex BN15 8UF
Tel: 01903 767800
www.airbrushes.com
*Airbrushes and equipment, paints and pigments (including
Lifecolor, Alclad2, Wilder and Darkstar)*

Albion Alloys
Spacemaker House, 518 Wallisdown Road,
Bournemouth BH11 8PT
Tel: 01202 511232
www.albionhobbies.com
Abrasives, modelling tools and equipment

Axminster Power Tool Centre
Unit 10 Weycroft Avenue, Axminster,
Devon EX13 5PH
Tel: 03332 406406
www.axminster.co.uk
Craft and hobby tools, abrasives

Eileen's Emporium
Unit 19.12 Highnam Business Centre, Newent Road,
Gloucester GL2 8DN
Tel: 01531 828009
www.eileensemporium.com
Tools, airbrushes, paints, adhesives and materials

Expo Tools
Unit 6, The Salterns, Tenby SA70 7NJ
Tel: 01834 845150
www.expotools.com
Tools, airbrushes, paints, paintbrushes, adhesives and materials

Howes Models
Unit 2C/D Station Field Ind. Est., Rowles Way,
Kidlington OX5 1LA
Tel: 01865 848000
www.howesmodels.co.uk
RailMatch paints

Just Like the Real Thing
26 Whittle Place, South Newmoor Industrial Estate,
Irvine KA11 4HR
Tel: 01294 222988
www.justliketherealthing.co.uk
Paints and modelling accessories

Modelmates
Tel: 07926 196471
www.modelmates.co.uk
Weathering dyes and Rust Effect fluids

Phoenix Precision Paints
Orwell Court, Wickford SS11 8YJ
Tel: 01268 730549
www.phoenix-paints.co.uk
Paints, thinners, masking and accessories

Precision Decals
Tel: 07800 744170
www.precisionlabels.com
*Transfers, included pre-faded/distressed logos for modern image
subjects, custom decal service*

Scale Model Shop
Tel: 01422 405040
www.scalemodelshop.co.uk
*Modelling tools, paints, washes, pigments and chipping fluids
(including Abteilung, Tamiya, Vallejo, AK Interactive and MIG)*

USEFUL WEBSITES

George Dent Model Maker: A Model Maker's Diary
http://georgedentmodelmaker.blogspot.com

Model Rail Magazine
www.model-rail.co.uk

RECOMMENDED VIEWING

The Model Rail Expert DVD series, featuring George Dent

The Weathering Expert

The Definitive Airbrush Expert

The Rolling Stock Weathering Expert

Telerail,
Royal Scot Suite,
Carnforth Station Heritage Centre
LA5 9TR
Tel: 01524 735774
www.telerail.co.uk

INDEX

aerosols   17, 36, 76
airbrush techniques   56–62, 66–71, 85–86, 107–108, 167–172, 178–179, 192–195, 198–199, 200–203
airbrushes   50–53, 63–64

brushes   22–23

chipping   91–93, 97–99, 100–101, 103, 130–131, 157, 197, 204–205
clear coats   17, 108, 111, 125, 141–142, 156, 180, 189–191, 203
colour modulation   111–113, 128–129, 166–173, 200–203
coloured pencils   11, 20, 34, 147–148, 181, 195–196
compressors   53–54

decals   104, 108, 111, 113, 165, 169
distressing   39–40, 95–96, 98, 101–102, 162–165, 203
dry-brushing   43–46, 49, 79, 85, 147, 156, 180
dyes   17–18, 83–84

fading   126–127, 136–137, 167–173
filters   102–104, 138–142, 155–157

grease effects   121, 133–134, 181–182

limescale   198–199

masking   26–28, 89–90, 93, 95, 115, 120–121, 167, 169, 175, 197

paint types   14–18
powders/pigments   19–20, 33–38, 42–43, 46, 74–78, 82, 87, 97, 115, 119, 145–146, 152–154 176–177, 184–185
preparation   24–26, 114–115, 132, 143, 174
pre-shading   12, 106–113, 171–173, 200–202

rust   12, 76, 79, 80–99, 127, 133–134, 170, 195–197, 203–205

shading   192–195
spattering   47–49
stencils   159, 164
streaking   170, 188–189

T-Cut   123–125, 160–161, 162–164, 169, 183, 185–187
texture   45–47, 72–73, 80–81, 88–89, 94, 96–99, 101–105, 115, 118–119, 137, 152–154, 185, 203–204
timber effects   39–43, 100–105
tinting   190–191
tools   21–24

washes   18–19, 30–33, 41–42, 65, 70, 76, 78, 85–86, 101, 103, 135–136, 143–144, 147–148, 158–159, 175–177, 180
weathering, reason for   7–10
wheels, cleaning   28–29, 134, 182
wiper trails   149–150

zero priming   109–111

ALSO BY GEORGE DENT

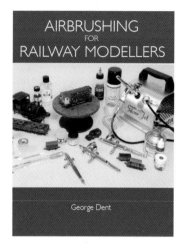

Airbrushing for Railway Modellers

ISBN 978 1 84797 265 1

224pp, 500 illustrations

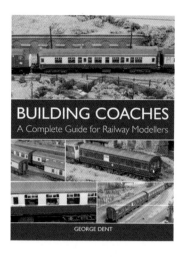

Building Coaches

ISBN 978 1 78500 205 2

256pp, 600 illustrations

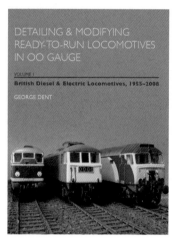

Detailing and Modifying Ready-to-Run Locomotives in OO Gauge Volume 1 – British Diesel & Electric Locomotives, 1955–2008

ISBN 978 1 84797 093 0

192pp, 390 illustrations

Detailing and Modifying Ready-to-Run Locomotives in OO Gauge Volume 2 – British Steam Locomotives, 1948–1968

ISBN 978 1 84797 145 6

192pp, 400 illustrations

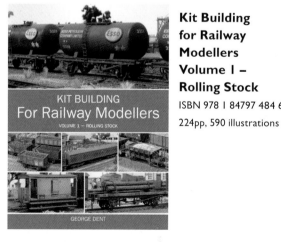

Kit Building for Railway Modellers Volume 1 – Rolling Stock

ISBN 978 1 84797 484 6

224pp, 590 illustrations

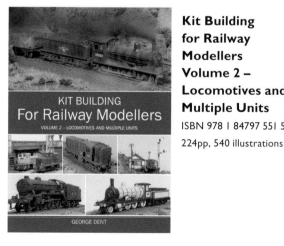

Kit Building for Railway Modellers Volume 2 – Locomotives and Multiple Units

ISBN 978 1 84797 551 5

224pp, 540 illustrations

www.crowood.com